Getting It
Together

Getting It Together:

A Psychology Book for Today's Problems

by Phyllis Anne Harrison, M.D.

 **Learning Trends**
A division of
GLOBE BOOK COMPANY, INC.
New York—Chicago—Dallas

AUTHOR

Phyllis Anne Harrison, M.D., a black woman, has served as pediatrician and child psychiatrist in New York City public and private schools, as well as in school systems in Florida, Georgia, Sweden, and Denmark. She is assistant clinical professor of pediatrics and psychiatry at the Albert Einstein College of Medicine, Bronx, New York, specifically working in The Children's Evaluation and Rehabilitation Clinic of The Rose Fitzgerald Kennedy Center for Research in Mental Retardation and Human Development.

A member of numerous commissions, Dr. Harrison also serves on the boards of several institutions of higher learning. President Nixon has appointed her to his Advisory Council on Drug Abuse. Her cable television program "All About Parents" is well known nationally.

CONSULTANT

Joseph M. Oxenhorn has served as science teacher, department head, and principal in several metropolitan school systems. He is the author of numerous books and technical manuals, including the celebrated *Pathways in Science* series.

ISBN: 0-87065-920-0

ACKNOWLEDGEMENTS

PHOTOGRAPHS:
Berne Greene: 10, 22, 70-71
Arthur Tress: 14-15, 96
James Carroll: 19, 91, 93, 152-153, 157
Geoffrey Gove: 29, 39, 47, 54, 59, 79, 102, 108, 116, 120, 137, 172
Harry Wilks: 30, 66, 161
Paolo Koch (Rapho Guillumette): 35
Circus World Museum, Baraboo, Wisconsin: 42
United Press International: 60, 126
James Smith: 77, 83, 87, 139, 148
Ken Heyman: 109, 115
American Cancer Society: 131, 133
Thomas Haar: 165
Photo Trends: 170
Daniel Nelkin: 52-53
Unations: 69
American Museum of Natural History: 171

DRAWINGS:
Bob Dole

Contents

This is a book about you.

You are as important as any other person in the world. Today's world is faced with a lot of problems that can be solved only by solving them for everybody. A black American leader—speaking to all Americans—once said, "If you're not part of the solution, then you're part of the problem." This book tries to help you become part of the solution.

Before you can command others, before you can lead others, before you can help others, you must be in command of yourself. To do this, you must learn about yourself. You learn about yourself so that you can like yourself. When this happens, you have self-respect. And with self-respect, you can become the person you were meant to be.

What does this book have to say about you?

UNIT I

It begins with a section on personality and psychology. Psychology is a subject that includes the development of people's personalities. This section discusses some of the problems that come into the lives of teen-agers. It suggests some ways you might handle these problems. Here, you can also find out how your emotions influence the development of your personality.

UNIT II

The second section of the book explains some physical facts about your body. This includes the intricate system which controls your growth, sex drive, and emotions. There is a definite relationship between your health and your personality. This section tells you what you can do to keep your body healthy so that your personality can develop normally.

UNIT III

Since your personality is often the way others see you, how you act with your friends is an important part of your personality. The third section of the book tries to straighten out some of the problems that you might have in meeting and getting to know others.

Understanding why other people act the way they do is also important. You can then have a better knowledge of how to act and how to react to behavior that might be puzzling. This section should help you form stronger friendships with the people you know now, and to make more friends in the future.

UNIT IV

The next section of the book is about those people you've known all your life—your family. How well have you known them? You've been close to them, loved them, and argued with them at times. Maybe at this stage of your life, you feel that they don't understand you as well as they used to.

And maybe they don't. But that's because you're on the way to becoming an adult, a more complicated person, certainly, and you aren't as easy to understand as you once were, even for your family. Helping others to understand the way you are and the ways you've changed is part of becoming an adult, too. This section tries to show you some ways to get along with your family while being true to yourself.

UNIT V

When people use the word "drugs" in connection with young people, they usually mean something bad. Yet practically everybody uses drugs of one kind or another, and most of the time they think nothing of it. But drugs can

8

cause problems. The next section of this book will try to give you some information that will help you toward your own solution to that problem. Of course, alcohol and nicotine are just as truly drugs as marijuana, cocaine, and amphetamines. All of these, and others, are discussed.

UNIT VI

The final section of the book is a guide to the sexuality you have developed lately, or will soon. It tells what kinds of changes have been taking place in your body that enable you to become a father or mother. This section also deals with the kinds of sexual expression that are possible, including some that you may not have thought of in quite that way before. There is a discussion of the development of love and what makes you ready for it—not just the growth spurt of your teen-age years, but an emotion that has been building in you since you were born.

Throughout *The Psychology of Growing Up*, there are study aids designed to increase your interest and understanding of the various topics that have been discussed in the chapters. The purpose of this book is to help guide your development so that you will grow into emotionally mature, happy, and fulfilled adults.

It's your book, and it's about you.

Unit I | The Whole Personality

Chapter 1
What Is Personality?

I'm Nobody
by Emily Dickinson

I'm nobody! Who are you?
Are you nobody, too?
Then there's a pair of us—don't tell!
They'd banish us, you know.

How dreary to be somebody!
How public, like a frog
To tell your name the livelong day
To an admiring bog!

Did you ever say about somebody, "I like his personality"? Or, "She has a nice personality"? Wasn't this the same as saying, "I like him"? Or, "She is a nice person"? Probably it was, even though you may not have thought about it that way, because the *personality* of a person is the way he is and behaves. It is the way he comes across to others. It is his outward appearance, and also a reflection of the way he feels inside.

What do you think the character in the Emily Dickinson poem thought his personality was like?

You can't separate the personality from the person. Your personality shows in everything that you do. Does this mean your personality never changes? No. For any number of reasons, you may act in a certain way one day and then very differently the next day. This is nothing to worry about, unless it begins to happen very often, or if the changes in your behavior seem to have no reason behind them.

Acting differently at different times is called *inconsistency*. We say that a person who changes his mind or his way of behaving for no good reason is *inconsistent*. Being inconsistent usually makes people who have to deal with us nervous. They don't know what to expect next. It is not a pleasing thing when it is part of a person's personality.

For example, a man may come home to his family every night and sit down to dinner relaxed and happy. He may tell stories and be interested about what happened to his wife and children all day. But one evening he comes home tense and irritable. He is angry at dinner, and complains about the least little thing. His family "catches" the tenseness from him, and wonders what is the matter. Everyone becomes upset.

How did you get your personality? Why do you act the way you do? There are two general causes that shape

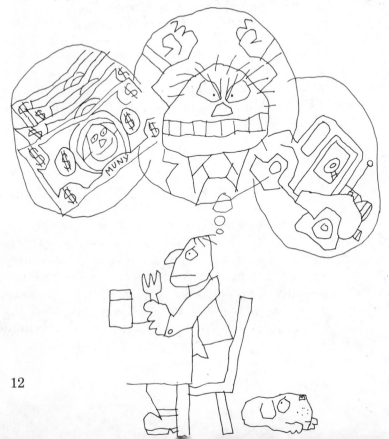

people's personalities. They are called *heredity* and *environment*.

Heredity is the way traits and characteristics of the parents are carried down to the next generation. Environment is the learning, or experience, that influences our personalities.

Whatever characteristics we got from our parents came to us through *heredity*. When someone says of a girl, for instance, "She looks just like her mother," they are talking about heredity. The girl's looks are *inherited* from her mother. In the same way, it might be noticeable that the girl has a hot temper, just like her father's. This also might be an inherited part of her personality.

Environment is all around us—people, places, and events which affect us, sometimes in ways we aren't aware of. If a man buys a used car which breaks down a month later, he will be more careful the next time he buys a car. He will be more suspicious. Maybe in the future he will continue to be more suspicious about other things as well. His personality will have changed because of his environment.

Which is more important in the development of personality, heredity or environment? Scientists have argued over this question for a long time. Even today there is no complete agreement on the answer. It is clear that they both play an important role.

How can you find out about your own personality? Where did it come from? Why should you care?

First of all, it is helpful to know how your personality developed so that you can change the parts of it that make you unhappy. For instance, a person who is very stubborn may have trouble getting along with people. If he wants, he can try to improve his personality by finding out why he acts so stubborn in the first place.

It is not unusual for people to want to act a certain way, and find that they go out and act just the opposite. They become disappointed in themselves. This is very common.

By studying your personality, you can understand yourself and the way you act. When you understand yourself, you will have better control over what you do and what happens to you.

Our personalities develop through learning. The environment is the teacher we learn from. If a baby cries, his mother comes to find out what is the matter. The baby soon makes the connection between crying and his mother coming to feed him, or change him, or hold him. He learns that crying is the way to get what he wants. He has learned a lesson from his environment.

The environment may be an unhealthy one, however. In that case, a child may learn behavior that will bring him trouble later in life. Suppose his mother is often busy with other things, and has little time to give him attention. The

child may find that the only way to get attention is to do something that will bring punishment, for example, pulling a lamp off a table. His environment is teaching him that the only way to be noticed is to do something for which he will be punished.

Now that you are older, not only your family but also your friends are very important to your environment. You look to your friends for guidance in how to dress and how to behave. There is security in doing what the group is doing. A term often used to describe a group of friends of about the same ages is a *peer group*.

Right now, the need to belong to a peer group, and to do the things it does, is strong. As you gain more and more security from acting within a group, you will get the confidence to strike out on your own.

Study Aids

The Vocabulary of Psychology

1. Each word in the left column has a definition in the right column. In your notebook write the number of the word at the left and match it with the letter of its definition.

1. personality	a. group of people of similar ages and interests
2. inconsistency	b. the carrying-down from parent to child of traits and characteristics
3. heredity	c. the way a person acts and appears to others
4. environment	d. the learning, or experiences, that cause some parts of our personalities
5. peer group	e. breaking a pattern of action for no apparent reason

2. Write the letters *a* through *g* in your notebook. Next to each letter write the word or words from question 1 that correctly belong in the blank space in each of the following statements. Some words will be used more than once.

a. Taking drugs at a party because your friends are doing it is acting according to the dictates of your

_____ .

b. Bill has the same color eyes as his father. It is part of his _____ .

c. Part of your _____ is the way you appear to other people.

d. All year long Carmen's mother came home in time to fix supper. Today she came home two hours late. There was an _____ in her behavior.

e. Through _____ a person may look like his parents.

f. The way other people act toward us is part of our _____ .

g. Many children living in California had nightmares for weeks after the earthquake there. This may have been a result of their _____ or their _____ .

II. Understanding Personality

Some of the statements that follow are incorrect. Rewrite the statements that are false to make them true. Do not simply insert words such as "not," "don't," "isn't," etc.

a. Your personality always remains the same.
b. Heredity and environment both affect the development of your personality.
c. Those parts of your personality that you learned came from your environment.
d. Science tells us that heredity is more important than environment in the development of personality.
e. If a baby cries, his mother should punish him.
f. Belonging to a peer group is a sign of maturity.
g. A person who breaks a regular pattern of behavior is being consistent.
h. Everything about our personalities is necessary and good.

17

III. *Talking It Over*

1. A teacher said, "I like to be strict one day, and easy the next. That way it keeps the students on their toes." What type of behavior is this? Tell whether you think the teacher's policy is a good one. Explain your views.

2. Give an example where belonging to a peer group is helpful and another where it is harmful. Discuss the personality of Tom who, throughout life, follows the crowd in dress and in everything else he does.

3. Recently a young teen-age boy was made to spend the night in the same jail cell in which his father had hanged himself years before. The experience was supposed to frighten him into being a good citizen, but in the morning it was found that he, too, had hanged himself. Was his action the result of heredity or environment? Explain.

Chapter 2
Your Emotions and Your Needs

Some writer or other is supposed to have said that human life is like an apartment in which all the doors are shut. You stand in a room and you can see that well enough. But you can't see what's in any of the other rooms. That's pretty much what I feel. How can I tell people answers to things they want to ask me when I can't even tell who I am? Everybody's always asking "What do you want to be?" How can you answer that? "Who are you?" is a better question.

Your feelings are part of your personality. We call these feelings *emotions*. Some emotions are happiness, anger, fear, love, and sadness. Sometimes emotions come upon you suddenly and make you want to act out what you feel—to cry, to laugh, to hit someone, to run away. Other times emotions may keep you from doing anything—boredom, contentment, and depression are emotions too.

Emotions are normal. They are good for you. Without emotions, life would be dull. A person who tries to hide his emotions soon finds the strain too hard to handle. Normal people show their emotions when they feel them.

On the other hand, we may not always be in situations where showing our emotions is acceptable. If a man gets angry at his boss, he cannot show anger by hitting his boss—not if he wants to keep his job. Sometimes we are in situations that make us afraid, and we feel like running away. But this may not be the best response. So we have to fight the fear, rather than run.

Teen-agers usually have very strong emotions. There are physical reasons for this. It is partly because they are developing sexually. They are growing and experiencing new ideas and actions. There seem to be so many new things they can try that they don't know where to start.

Just like adults, teen-agers can run into problems if they act on their emotions immediately. For example, you might feel so good when you get behind the wheel of a car that you want to drive it as fast as it will go. The feeling is normal, yet the consequences of acting on the feeling can be disastrous.

Much has been written about the "generation gap." Teen-agers have a natural desire to be independent, to try things on their own, to make their own decisions. If they didn't do these things, they would never become mature adults.

Yet their parents worry about them. Older people's emotions are more controllable and set than teen-agers. They prefer their environment to be more consistent, and

20

often forget the strong needs that they had when younger. Older people have learned about mistakes they have made, and they want to protect their children from making what they think are the same mistakes. The problem is, however, that it is necessary to make mistakes in order to learn. But teen-agers often resent their parents' protectiveness.

What the generation gap is all about is a conflict of emotions. Parents who love their children want to protect them. They see the danger in some of the things teen-agers do and are afraid they will get hurt. These parents feel the emotions of love, protectiveness, and fear.

Unfortunately, these feelings conflict with the emotions felt by their children. Teen-agers are curious, impulsive, and impatient. They want to test the limits of things because they want to test themselves. They sometimes play music at full volume, drive cars at top speed, and exert their bodies to the point of exhaustion. Older people have already established limits for themselves, and are not always sympathetic to teen-agers who are trying to find their own.

As you can see, different people feel different emotions toward the same things. This is because people have different kinds of *emotional needs*. Just as the body has physical needs, such as food, water, warmth, and sleep, so does the personality. The needs of the personality are called emotional needs. When the body is lacking in its physical needs, it can get sick. So can the personality, if deprived of its needs.

Some emotional needs are *affection*, *security*, *achievement*, and *self-esteem*. Affection is the feeling of being loved. Security is feeling safe from danger. Achievement is the sense of working for a purpose. Self-esteem is the feeling of one's own value.

Affection is the first emotional need that a person has. Babies that do not get regular affection can become emotionally and even physically unhealthy as a result. As you get older, you need to have friends to develop your

personality. A person who grew up with no friends would not be able to get along in society. Finally, you will fall in love. One person will appeal to you in a special way. The two of you will have a relationship in which both of you will reinforce the other with affection.

Security is closely related to affection. A baby is secure if he knows that someone will come when he cries. He must know he will be fed and kept warm. Little children gradually develop less of a dependence on their parents, but they need the feeling that their parents are there to help if danger arises. Even older children and teen-agers need the assurance of home and parents. This is why broken homes or the death of a parent sometimes cause emotional problems. Adults, too, need security. They may get it from the affection and respect of their husband or wife. They may get it from a steady, well-paying job. They may even get it from owning a house or a business or a car.

Security in adults is obviously similar to achievement, another emotional need. When we were younger, the need for achievement helped us to learn how to do very simple things, such as walking and talking. Later, achievement takes different forms in different people. Some people may enjoy playing football, and some would rather draw pictures, but the need to do things well is there.

Doing anything well is one way to achieve self-esteem. Self-esteem means simply to be content with yourself, proud of the way you are and the way you act toward others. This doesn't mean that there can't be things about you that you would like to change. Practically everyone wishes there were something a little different about himself or herself. People change the color of their hair, buy stylish pairs of glasses, put braces on their teeth and try to take off weight in an attempt to look better. But they may still have a high self-esteem.

 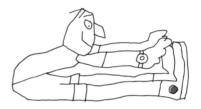

It is when people confuse good looks, high intelligence, athletic ability, or some other quality with self-esteem that trouble results. The fact is that everybody has some desirable qualities that can be developed. It does no good to wish for something that you weren't born with and can't achieve by hard work or practice.

Something anyone can have is a good personality. Self-esteem is an essential part of a good personality. If you don't like yourself, others will sense there's something wrong with you.

Does this mean you should try to develop a good personality by doing the things others tell you are worthwhile? No. *You* must choose what you want to accomplish. *You* must choose what kind of person you want to be. *You* must choose what qualities you are capable of developing. This book cannot say what kind of person you should be. Neither can your parents or teachers. They can point out things to you and try to help you make the right decisions. But the person you become depends on you. It must be a person you will like.

Study Aids

I. The Vocabulary of Psychology

1. Each word in the left column has a definition in the right column. In your notebook write the number of the word on the left and match it with the letter of its definition.

1. emotions	a. the feeling of being loved
2. affection	b. feelings that are part of our personalities
3. security	c. being content with and proud of yourself
4. achievement	d. the feeling of being safe
5. self-esteem	e. the feeling of having done something worthwhile

2. Write the letters *a* through *f* in your notebook. Next to each letter write the word or words from question 1 that correctly belong in the blank spaces in each of the following statements. Some words will be used more than once.

a. Your _____ will cause you to act in different ways at different times.

b. _____ is the feeling that what we have done is worthwhile.

c. When a baby's mother and father pick him up and rock him, his need for _____ is being satisfied.

d. When a small child gets lost in a department store, he may begin to cry. He has lost his sense of

_____ .

e. A person who says, "I'm too dumb to do well in school. I'm not even going to study," is probably lacking in _____ .

f. Cleaning your classroom or your room at home can give you a sense of _____ .

II. *Understanding Your Emotions and Your Needs*

Some of the statements that follow are incorrect. Rewrite the setences that are false to make them true. Do not simply insert words such as "not," "don't," "isn't," etc.

    a. Doing well what you enjoy is one way to achieve self-esteem.

    b. Anyone can have a good personality.

    c. The need for security is a physical need.

    d. Teen-agers, because of their youth, find it easier to control their emotions.

    e. Everybody has some desirable qualities that can be developed.

    f. The first emotional need in a person's life is the need for achievement.

    g. Everybody makes mistakes, but mistakes help us learn.

III. *Talking It Over*

1. After the earthquake in Los Angeles, psychologists found that what frightened children most was not the earthquake itself, but the fact that they could see that their parents were afraid. Why would this be, according to what you have read in the chapter?

2. In California recently, the newspapers reported the story of a man who had been a great baseball player in high school and college. He was signed by the Los Angeles Dodgers but was never called up from the minor leagues. One night he went to a college field where he had pitched a no-hitter, set all his trophies and awards around him on the pitcher's mound, and shot himself. What would you say about that man's sense of self-esteem? Was it based on something that was permanent? If the man came to you for help, what would you have told him?

3. How can knowing about emotions help us get along with people?

Chapter 3
Conflict:
Causes, Reactions, Solutions

Dorcas was pouring out cornflakes when her father came back. . . . On his hand sat the biggest grasshopper Dorcas had ever seen. Her father held the huge thing practically under her nose.

"See? I found him in the alley this morning, and I thought maybe you could take him to biology class." . . .

Dorcas tried to smile. "All right, Daddy. And thank you very much. What shall we do with him now?"

"I'll get a jar. Where's a jar?" He was already on his way to the basement.

Riding to school with her father, Dorcas watched the grasshopper jumping frantically inside the glass container. . . .

Dorcas felt tears come to her eyes, and she turned her face to the window so that her father wouldn't notice. She didn't even know if the teacher wanted them to bring things for observation. After all, it was only the second day of school, and—she sighed. Her father was always so enthusiastic. Actually, in some ways he was very like a small boy.

But she loved him, and she wouldn't have hurt his feelings for anything. She was cheerful as she got out of the car. . . .

The car roared off, and Dorcas hurried into the school, balancing the jar on top of her books. It was a lucky thing biology was her first class. She wouldn't have to look at the jar and the frantic thing inside it for very much longer now.

The bell rang, and Dorcas walked slowly toward the biology room. What could she do? A thought flashed into her mind. Of course! She'd simply let the grasshopper go! She pictured herself walking out to the playground, uncapping the jar. She saw the grasshopper's spiky legs propel him slowly out of his prison, and she watched him leap away in great joyous hops.

But she had reached the door of the biology room. She looked down at the grasshopper, quiet now in his glass cage, and silently apologized to him. She couldn't let him go, of course. There would be questions at home, Daddy would be hurt . . . .

Dorcas squared her shoulders and walked through the door. She felt nearly as trapped as the grasshopper.

Adapted and reprinted by permission from *Literary Cavalcade,* © by Scholastic Magazines, Inc.

The period of your life when you begin to develop in a sexual way is called *puberty.* This does not happen to everyone at the same age. Puberty usually takes place between the ages of 11 and 16, but sometimes a little earlier or later. Puberty, along with the period just afterward, is also called *adolescence.* During this time, you learn how to develop your capabilities as men and women. You find your strengths, learn to cope with your shortcomings, and find a variety of new interests.

Because sexual emotions are so strong and unfamiliar at this time, many teen-agers, or adolescents, have trouble handling the problems that sexual development and growing up bring. This kind of trouble is called a *conflict.* A conflict is like a battle inside you between two opposing ideas or feelings or needs.

People experience conflicts all the time, not only in sexual matters. Suppose two of your friends had a fight and weren't speaking to each other, and they both wanted you to go out with them on Friday night. You might have to decide which of them you wanted to go out with. You would have a conflict over which of them you liked better.

We can have conflicts about our relationships with our parents and other members of our families. Suppose your mother is the only person in the family who works and she leaves home at seven in the morning and doesn't return home until eight in the evening. You have planned to go to the recreational center to play basketball, and she asks you to take your younger brother and sister along so that she can have some quiet around the house.

Along with this, your mother does not notice the drawing that you made in school that day and had really wanted her to admire. You feel obligated to help your mother, but you are a bit angry with her because she just mumbled about the drawing. Worse yet, you don't want to be bothered with your younger brother and sister because you want to meet with your friends and talk about your own affairs.

It is normal to feel annoyance and anger in a situation like this. The problem is how to solve the situation so that everyone is just a little bit satisfied. You could quietly tell your mother about your hurt feelings about the drawing. Further, you could tell your mother that taking along your younger brother and sister would be a bother, and why. Perhaps a *compromise* could be worked out. A compromise is a way of settling a disagreement in which both sides

give in a little. For example, you could agree with your
mother to take your brother and sister for an hour. After she
had some time to get herself together, you could bring them
home and go back with your friends for the rest of the
evening.

Conflicts over sexual matters are also very common, particularly during adolescence. At this time, you are
faced with social situations with which you may have had
little experience. Suppose a girl likes a boy as a friend, but
not in a sexual way. If the boy liked her in a romantic, or
sexual way, there would be a conflict between the two ways
they wanted to treat each other.

It's hard to deal with this sort of conflict because it
would be hard to find a solution that wouldn't cause one or
both of the people to be hurt. The girl might tell the boy that
she is going steady with somebody else. But if he found out
that she wasn't, he would think she told him that because
she didn't like him. Another possibility is that the girl might
decide to let the boy think she liked him in a sexual way.
But, this might lead to their doing things she wasn't ready

to do and she didn't enjoy, but had to pretend she did. Also, if other people thought she was going steady with this boy, she might not be asked out by people she liked better.

Or a boy may not be interested as yet in any particular girl. But the other boys he knows are dating. To be with them, he tries to sell himself the idea that he likes a certain girl, and the girl he picks gets too interested in him. He is suddenly a lot more involved than he wants to be.

How can we solve problems like these? Part of the answer comes in understanding what we, as individual human beings, should be looking for to make us happy.

Happiness is the result of leading a balanced life so that all our needs are met. These needs include physical and emotional ones.

An emotional need which is quite strong in adolescence is security. Often a young person will agree to go steady more out of a need to have a boyfriend or a girlfriend than because the other person is genuinely appealing. Suppose a boy calls a girl and asks her to go out to a discotheque. She might agree to go, even though she knows he asked a friend of hers the day before and was turned down, and even though she doesn't particularly like this boy. What she wants is to go to the discotheque instead of staying home. However, she might still have a dull time at the discotheque, and wonder why.

Another girl might tell one of her girl friends that she will go to the movies with her on Saturday. The next day a boy at school asks her to go to the movies with him. She would rather go to the movie with this boy, but has already told her girl friend, who doesn't have many dates with boys, that she will go with her. So what should she do? If she goes with the boy, her girl friend will be hurt. On the other hand, this boy might think she is putting him down if she says she can't go, and he might not ask her out again.

As you can see, sometimes conflicts come up that don't have solutions that will be perfectly satisfactory. The important thing to remember is that you should make the best decision you can, and then not regret it or feel guilty about what might happen. Sometimes it's not possible to avoid hurting others, particularly if their feeling toward us is different from our feelings toward them. Nobody makes the right decision all the time, but if you have made what you thought was a good decision, you have done what you thought was right and you should not feel sorry about it.

Here are some guidelines that may help you to make a good decision:

1. Understand what the conflict is.

2. Decide what the possible solutions or answers are.

3. Think what the results of each solution would be.

4. Ask for advice from people you trust, especially someone who is likely to have experienced similar problems, or who seems to have made good decisions in solving other kinds of problems.

5. Be open about your solution. Do not be ashamed to tell anyone what you have decided.

6. Know the reasons for your decision; make sure you understand why you made it.

7. Do what you have decided.

8. Don't feel guilty afterwards if you think you have made the wrong decision.

Study Aids

The Vocabulary of Psychology

1. Each word in the left column has a definition in the right column. In your notebook write the number of the word on the left and match it with the letter of its definition.

1. puberty	a. a battle inside yourself
2. adolescence	b. another name for puberty
3. conflict	c. a way of settling a disagreement in which both sides give in a little
4. compromise	d. the time of your life when you mature physically

2. Write the letters *a* through *d* in your notebook. Next to each letter write the word or words from question 1 that correctly belong in the blank space in each of the following statements.

   a. _____ is the time when we find strengths and new interests.

   b. Mature people often seek a _____ as a way of settling disagreements.

   c. _____ is the time of your life when you become capable of sexual activity.

   d. Trying to handle two opposing emotions can produce a _____ .

II. *Understanding Conflict: Causes, Reactions, Solutions*

Some of the statements that follow are incorrect. Rewrite the sentences that are false to make them true. Do not simply insert words such as "not," "don't," "isn't," etc.

   a. A conflict is like a battle within you over two or more ways you might act.

b. Adolescence is a time for finding out your strengths.

c. It is impossible to say what kinds of things may make us happy.

d. If two people having an argument decide to give in a little on both sides to settle it, they are making a compromise.

e. The emotional need for security is weak during adolescence.

f. After you have made a decision as to how to solve a conflict, you should wait before carrying it out.

III. *Talking It Over*

1. Why is it important not to feel guilty after you have made your decision and acted upon it? Suppose you accidentally hurt somebody through what you have done?

2. A pro football player was asked by a reporter if he had become upset during a game in which he had dropped a touchdown pass. The football player replied that he had forgotten about it by the time he came back to the huddle. Was this a good attitude? For what reason?

3. Maria was a good student and found it easy to do her homework. Her boyfriend, Paul, would copy her answers in the morning before class. She didn't think this was right, but let him do it because she was afraid he would drop her. One day the teacher told Maria he knew she was helping Paul to cheat. The next day, she wouldn't let Paul have her homework. He got angry and asked another girl to go out on Friday night. When Maria heard about this, she started playing up to Jack, another boy in the class. She didn't care much for Jack, but knew he had always liked her and she wanted to show Paul that she didn't need him anymore.

Discuss the decisions Maria made in the preceding paragraph. Where were the conflicts? Did she see all of them? Would she have done anything differently if she had used the eight guidelines at the end of this chapter?

Chapter 4
Personality Habits

He would tell me things like, "Claude, you're being pessimistic, and this is one way to lose out on anything. Did I ever tell you about two frogs who were sitting up on a milk vat and fell in?"

I said, "No, you never told me."

He said, "Well, there were two frogs sitting on a milk vat one time. The frogs fell into the milk vat. It was very deep. They kept swimming and swimming around, and they couldn't get out. They couldn't climb out because they were too far down. One frog said, 'Oh, I can't make it, and I'm going to give up.' And the other frog kept swimming and swimming. His arms became more and more tired, and it was harder and harder and harder for him to swim. Then he couldn't do another stroke. He couldn't throw one more arm into the milk. He kept trying and trying; it seemed as if the milk was getting hard and heavy. He kept trying; he knows that he's going to die, but as long as he's got this little bit of life in him, he's going to keep on swimming. On his last stroke, it seemed as though he had to pull a whole ocean back, but he did it and found himself sitting on top of a vat of butter."

I'll always remember that story.

Manchild in the Promised Land, by Claude Brown (copyright © Claude Brown 1965)

Now is the time when you can start to form good mental health habits. The next time you have a disappointment, think about it before you start getting upset. What caused the disappointment? Was it something you could

34

have prevented beforehand? Was it something that you couldn't do anything about?

For instance, if, on the day you plan to go on a picnic, it rains, you obviously can't help it. What can you do? Should you and your friends just go home and do nothing? Should you invite the gang to your house for the picnic? What if your house is not big enough, or your mother has said that she will not allow you to have a party there today? What if all your friends are in the same boat? It's too late to do anything. The next time you plan a picnic, you might try making an alternate plan in case of bad weather.

Too much of some emotions is destructive. One of the possibly dangerous emotions is *anxiety*. Anxiety is the feeling of nagging worry. A little anxiety can spur you on, make you work harder to accomplish a task. But too much anxiety can be a negative force in your life. If you always feel tense and worried, you will not be able to do your best. In fact, you may not be able to do anything. If you give in and let yourself be beaten by anxiety, you may rob yourself of the satisfaction of the vital psychological need for accomplishment and independence (security).

Knowing you can do something on your own, whether it is riding a bicycle, cheering up someone who is down, baking a cake, or buying a new outfit, is a psychological need. Anxiety that prevents you from filling your needs can drain your life. If you always have butterflies in your stomach, that's a sign of anxiety. If it is preventing you from doing your best, you should see your school guidance counselor for help. Anxiety can go away with help.

What should you do if you find yourself worrying all the time about something that hasn't happened or might not happen? For instance, what if you worry about getting sick? Worry is not a preventative medicine, like a polio shot. You should take care of your health as far as you reasonably can. Then, you should forget it. Find something else to think about. Visit friends. Find a hobby. Go to the movies.

What if you feel that you can't get angry without losing your self-control? Sometimes people are afraid to get angry for this reason. But if you try to pretend that you are not angry when you are, you may become physically or emotionally ill. You must admit your anger and allow it an outlet without losing control of yourself.

You can try to work off your anger in physical activity. If something has been bothering you for a long time, you can talk over the problem with some other person to get a fresh viewpoint. Above all, you should understand in your own mind why you are angry. If it is because of the actions of someone else, you should try to understand why the other person behaves as he does.

When a person becomes angry and finds that he cannot take out his anger on the person or thing that has made him angry, he will sometimes take it out on other people, including himself. If a person hates his job and his boss, yet stays for the money, he may come home and be cruel to his children. He may go out and get drunk. Activities like these, of course, don't solve the problem. The solution would come in trying to find another job or in working out peaceably whatever the trouble is at the present job.

Slamming your fist into a wall helps nothing, although a number of people do this or something similar when they are angry. It is better than slamming your fist into another person. Of course, once in a while, everyone is entitled to let off steam. The problem comes when you make a habit of doing this.

There is a famous cartoon by Charles Schulz, the creator of "Peanuts," in which Charlie Brown holds up a big sign that reads, "NO problem is so big or so overwhelming that it can't be run away from." We laugh at this because sometimes we all try to run away from our problems. Each of us needs to get away, to take a vacation, or go to the movies or a basketball game. But there is a difference between ignoring a problem for an hour or a few days and running away from it completely.

If you follow the steps for decision making in Chapter 3, however, you will find that you have adopted the habit of solving problems and dropped the habit of running

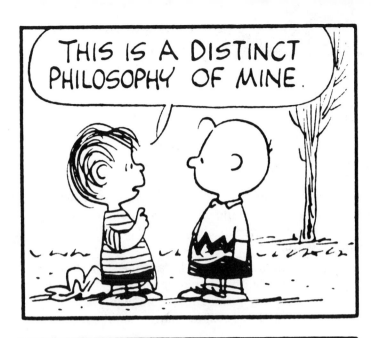

away from them. Remember, solving a problem to the best of your ability is better than brooding over it.

Study Aids

I. The Vocabulary of Psychology

In each group of three words, two of the words have almost the same meaning. In your notebook write the number of the word group and the letters that identify the two similar words.

1.   a. characteristic   b. tantrum   c. trait
2.   a. situation   b. circumstances   c. solution
3.   a. anxiety   b. anger   c. worry
4.   a. emotion   b. feeling   c. influence

II. Understanding Personality Habits

Some of the statements that follow are incorrect. Rewrite the sentences that are false to make them true. Do not simply insert words such as "not," "don't," "isn't," etc.

a. Too much of some emotions can be harmful.

b. When you are angry at someone, it can be helpful to understand why he acts the way he does.

c. When you feel yourself getting angry, you should fight it down.

d. The best thing to do about problems is to avoid them when they arise.

e. There is no sense in worrying about disappointments if there was nothing you could have done to avoid them.

f. Anxiety can sometimes be a good thing.

g. Physical activity can sometimes work off your anger.

III. Talking It Over

1. Certain jobs seem very dangerous. Washing windows on skyscraper buildings, construction work on new office buildings, stoking the furnaces in a steel mill, are all examples. Can you think of any others? How do you suppose the people in these jobs handle the pressure? Would these jobs be likely to cause anxiety in some people? Discuss.

2. Prizefighters, football players, and other sports figures engage in violent physical contact which would cause many people to lose their tempers. What would happen to a sports figure who lost his temper during a contest (even if he were not called for fouling)? Would he be able to perform as capably? Why or why not? How do you think these players manage to keep their tempers?

3. Besides anger, another emotion that people try to hide is sorrow. On a television program some time ago, an interview with a medical officer in Vietnam was shown. He said that he had seen so many terrible things in war that he no longer felt emotion. He told of hearing about the death of his mother and his young son in an automobile accident. He said he felt nothing when he heard the news. Was this a normal reaction? Was it a good or bad reaction? How can people like this be helped? Should they be? Why or why not?

Unit II | Your Body

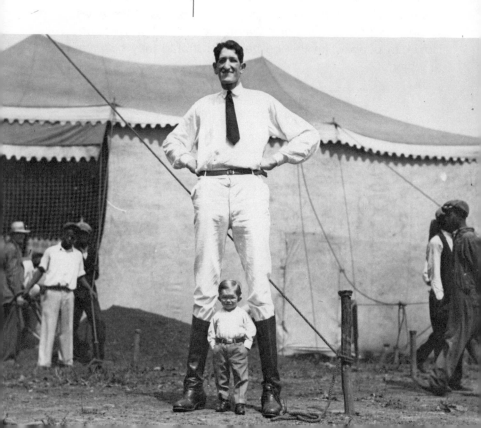

Chapter 1
Your Body's Messenger Systems

The Pituitary Gland.

(pi-tōo'-i-ter'-ē) *This gland has been called the master gland. It produces several hormones. Some of them act on other endocrine glands and cause them to produce hormones.*

How tall we are, or how short we are, has a lot to do with the the height of our parents and grandparents—with our heredity, and with what we eat and the amount of sleep we get—with our environment. But one of the pituitary hormones regulates our rate of growth.

Another one of the hormones the pituitary gland produces causes a mother who has just given birth to begin producing milk for her baby.

You have read something about how the human personality works. You know that how you look and feel affects your personality. You should also know that *how* you express your personality has something to do with your body as well.

Your movements and thoughts are coordinated by your *nervous system*. This consists of your brain, your spinal cord, and the various nerves and branches that extend throughout the body. All these nerves carry messages to the brain or from the brain. They may carry a message like, "Somebody is touching me," to the brain. And the brain may send a message through the system like, "Make a fist and move your arm."

The body has another communications system. This one is called the *endocrine system*. The endocrine system is a network of *glands*, or containers, that hold certain chemicals that can change the way the body works. These chemicals are called *hormones*. When they are released by the glands, hormones can cause different reactions in the body. One of these reactions is adolescence.

During adolescence, hormones are released by your endocrine glands that cause the changes some of you have already observed in your own bodies. The hormones are changing you from boys and girls into men and women.

The principal endocrine glands are: 1) the pituitary gland, 2) the adrenal glands, 3) the thyroid gland, 4) the parathyroid glands, 5) the sex glands, 6) the pancreas, and 7) the thymus gland.

The Pituitary Gland. This gland has been called the master gland. It produces several hormones. Some of them act on other endocrine glands and cause them to produce hormones.

How tall we are, or how short we are, has a lot to do with the height of our parents and grandparents—with our heredity, and with what we eat and the amount of sleep we get—with our environment. But one of the pituitary hormones regulates our rate of growth.

Another one of the hormones the pituitary gland produces causes a mother who has just given birth to begin producing milk for her baby.

The Adrenal Glands. There are two of these, one on top of each of your kidneys. The adrenal glands produce a hormone called adrenaline. This is the "emergency" hormone. It helps your body to respond powerfully in certain

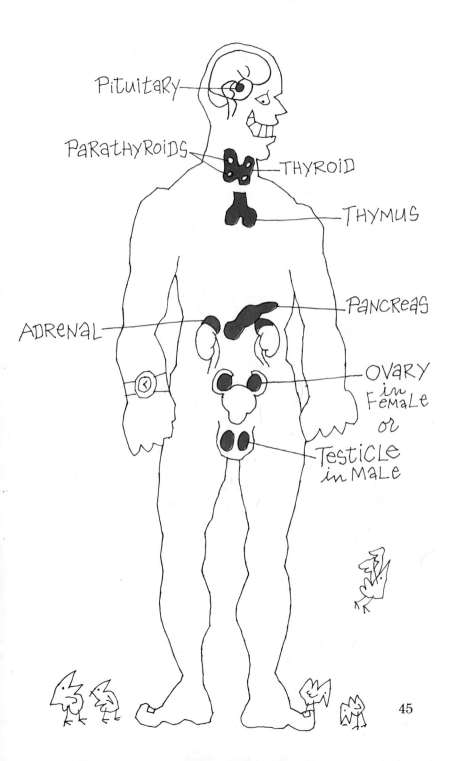

PituiTary

ParaThyRoiDs

THYROID

THYMUS

PANCReaS

ADRENAL

OVaRY
in
FemaLe
or
TesTiCLe
in MaLe

45

situations. It works by forcing the blood away from the digestive system into the brain and muscles.

Let us say that you are sitting and eating lunch. In the next room your younger brother and sister are sleeping. They are three and four years old. Suddenly you smell smoke. You rush in and find that there is a fire in their bedroom. Your adrenal glands start to send adrenaline into your bloodstream. The blood rushes from your stomach to your brain and muscles. Your heart begins to beat faster. Your hands become moist. The processes of digestion, which had begun, stop. You think quickly. You decide that the best thing to do is climb down the fire escape, carrying the two younger children. Ordinarily, you might not be able to lift both of them at one time, but your muscles have extra strength now because of the additional blood. You are able to do things that you might ordinarily be too slow or too weak to do.

The adrenal glands also produce a large number of hormones that are called *steroids*. Some of these cause the development of secondary sex characteristics in men and women. Body hair, the enlargement of the Adam's apple in boys, and the development of breasts in girls are all secondary sex characteristics.

The Thyroid Gland. This gland is located in the neck. It controls the rate at which your body turns food into energy. A person with too much thyroid hormone will be thin and nervous. A person with too little will be fat and sluggish. If the thyroid is damaged early in life, the individual might not develop normally, physically and mentally. Normal intelligence might be absent.

The Parathyroid Glands. These are small glands next to the thyroid. They act to control the body's use of calcium. If the parathyroids are lacking, the muscles do not function properly.

The Sex Glands. In females, these are the ovaries. In males, they are the testes. The ovaries produce *eggs* which

46

combine with the *sperm* produced by the testes to make a new human being. Both male and female sex glands also produce hormones that affect the secondary sex characteristics.

The Pancreas. The pancreas is located near the stomach. One of the most important hormones it produces is *insulin.* Insulin is necessary to the body's health. If there is not enough of it, a condition called *diabetes* results. This illness requires regular doses of insulin.

The Thymus. This is a gland which is comparatively large in infants. As the child grows, however, the gland gradually gets smaller. Scientists think that the thymus plays a part in growth and development. It may also have something to do with the way the body fights some diseases and becomes immune to certain others.

The entire endocrine system matures when the rest of your body does—that is, during adolescence. During this period of growth, there are some imbalances. Too much of one hormone may be produced, or not enough of another. Some doctors believe that acne, so common among teenagers, is the result of an endocrine hormone imbalance.

For the first time, the sex glands are sending their hormones into your bloodstream. The sex hormones and others have an effect on your emotions. As a result, your emotions are stronger now than they were before. Not only that, they are stronger than they will be after adolescence. The study of the way your body works can give you a better understanding of your feelings and emotions.

Study Aids

I. *The Vocabulary of Psychology*

Each word or phrase in the left column has a definition in the right column. In your notebook write the number of the word or phrase on the left and match it with the letter of its definition.

1. nervous system
2. endocrine system
3. glands
4. hormones
5. pituitary gland
6. adrenal gland
7. adrenaline
8. steroids
9. thyroid gland
10. parathyroid glands
11. sex glands
12. pancreas
13. insulin
14. diabetes
15. thymus gland

a. the endocrine gland that produces insulin
b. the gland that controls the rate at which the body turns food into energy
c. hormones that cause the development of secondary sex characteristics
d. an endocrine gland that gets smaller as the body grows
e. an illness that results from a shortage of insulin
f. the endocrine gland, sometimes called the master gland, that causes other glands to work
g. a network of glands that holds certain chemicals that can change the way your body works
h. together: your brain, spinal cord, and various nerves and branches extend throughout your body
i. small glands located next to the thyroid gland
j. containers in your body that hold chemicals
k. a hormone produced by the pancreas
l. glands that are called ovaries in females, testes in males
m. chemicals held in glands that can change the way the body works
n. glands that are found on top of your kidneys
o. a hormone that helps your body respond to crisis situations

II. *Talking It Over*

The state of your body's health can affect your mental attitude. When you have a cold, you may feel crabby and impatient. Why do you think this is? After a good meal, you may want to relax and enjoy conversation instead of studying. Why? Discuss the ways in which the workings of your glands might affect your personality. Could a physical injury do harm to your personality? How?

Chapter 2
Your Nervous System

It was on an October evening when I happened to go over to Jeff Stoneymaker's farm and first saw him lifting up the young heifer. . . .

"I know where you can pick up a scale real cheap," I said. "Used to belong to a veterinarian."

"Oh, I wasn't trying to figure the heifer's weight," Jeff said. . . .

. . . About a week later I dropped in on Jeff . . . . I noticed, as we sat in the parlor, that he kept looking at the clock on the mantelpiece. Finally, Jeff got up and said, "It's five o'clock. I'll have to leave you for a minute. I'll be right back."

Jeff went into the kitchen and then out of the back door. I guess I was curious because I went to the kitchen window and watched. He went over near the well. The heifer was there, near her mother. Jeff put his arms around the calf and lifted her up. Then he promptly put her down and started back toward the house.

When he got into the house again, I said to him, "Say, Jeff, why did you pick that heifer up?"

"I do it every evening," he said. "Exactly at five o'clock."

I asked him why.

"I've been doing it for about three weeks now—ever since the heifer was born."

"But how come?" I asked.

"Well, it's like this," he said. "Just like people, there is hardly any difference in an animal's size from day to day. So if I pick up the heifer at five

today, there's no reason why I shouldn't pick her up at five tomorrow."

"I'll grant you that," I said.

"Well," he said, "then if I keep it up—picking the heifer up every day without miss—then I ought to be able to pick her up when she's a full-grown cow." . . .

While your endocrine system is a kind of inside communication system, you also have an outside communication system. This is called the *nervous system*. The nervous system is organized into three main parts: the *central nervous system*, consisting of the brain (the communications center), the spinal cord (the main line of the system), and nerves; the *autonomic nervous system*; and the *sense organs*.

The central nervous system controls thought, memory, and voluntary action. Nerves are attached to the spinal cord and brain, and send messages to them. When you reach out your hand for a piece of cake, the action is controlled by nerve impulses or messages from the brain to the hand. This is a *voluntary* action, because you want it to happen.

Other actions are performed by the body without us having to think about them. These are *involuntary* actions. These actions, which include breathing, digestion, and heartbeat, are controlled by the *autonomic nervous system.*

The sense organs are: the eyes, the ears, the nose, the taste buds, and the skin. They are specialized to receive messages from the outside.

Certain actions that begin as part of your voluntary nervous system can become part of the autonomic nervous system. Learning how to ride a bike, for example, is difficult at first, and your body must strain to combine all the activi-

ties necessary. Later, however, these actions become automatic, and you can do them without effort.

Our mental responses are the same as our physical ones in this way. We can learn responses so that they become automatic. Remembering a new phone number is a good example. At first, we may have to write it down and make an effort to remember it, but as we use it more and more often, we can remember it easily.

Sometimes we form mental or physical habits that we may want to change. This, too, is possible. Our autonomic nervous system can be changed and influenced by conscious effort. This is the reason why athletes, even pro-

fessional athletes who have played for years, continue to practice constantly. The same is true of musicians, dancers, and anyone else who depends on a physical skill.

Suppose you want to form the habit of getting up at 7 a.m. If you are used to getting up an hour or so later, it will be hard for you at first, but you can provide artificial aids: an alarm clock, leaving the shades up in your room, etc. Soon you will find that you have formed the habit of getting up at 7 a.m. and you no longer need the artificial aids. The same is true of changes you may want to make in the way you speak to or act toward other people. Parts of our personalities are habits that can be changed.

SeMi-SuRe-FiRe ALaRM SYSTeM

SuN ① rises and melts ICe ②, causing FooT ③ to drop onto tail of COWARDLY WATCHDOG ④. Dog, thinking a burglar has stepped on his tail, runs under BED ⑤, pulling HooD ⑥ from head of RooSTeR ⑦. Rooster sees Sun ① and crows, rousing sleeper ⑧.

Study Aids

I. The Vocabulary of Psychology

1. Each word or phrase in the left column has a defition in the right column. In your notebook write the number of the word or phrase on the left and match it with the letter of its definition.

1. nervous system

2. voluntary

3. autonomic

4. sense organs

5. nerves

a. an action of this kind is one that you *want* to happen

b. these carry messages to the brain and spinal cord

c. this is part of the nervous system that causes actions that you don't think about to be performed

d. the outside communications system of your body

e. these are specialized to receive messages from the outside

2. Write the letters *a* through *e* in your notebook. Next to each letter write the word or words from question 1 that correctly belong in the blank space in each of the following statements.

a. A person watching a football game on television is using one of his _____ .

b. Impulses, or messages, are carried by _____ .

c. The central nervous system, autonomic nervous system, and sense organs are together called the

_____ .

d. When we hear an alarm bell, our hearts may beat faster. This is caused by the _____ nervous system.

e. When you walk in line to get out of the building during a fire drill, you are performing a _____ action.

II. *Understanding Your Nervous System*

Some of the statements that follow are incorrect. Rewrite the sentences that are false to make them true. Do not simply insert words such as "not," "don't," "isn't," etc.

a. You can change habits that have been formed within your nervous system.

b. The autonomic nervous system controls your heartbeat, breathing, digestion, and arm movements.

c. A good athlete seldom has to practice once he has learned his skills.

d. The five senses are hearing, taste, smell, action, and touch.

III. *Talking It Over*

1. Your nerves can respond in unpleasant ways to outside messages. A person who is under a great deal of stress may develop an upset stomach, ulcers, or serious illnesses. What part of the nervous system do you think controls this sort of reaction? Explain your answer.

2. Ways of dealing with situations become habits. If a person finds as a child that he can get away with unpleasant situations by making excuses, he may grow up making excuses every time he gets in trouble. Eventually, the attitude of such a person may be that everything unpleasant that happens is the fault of somebody or something else. How can a personality habit like this one be changed? Why would it be helpful to change it?

Chapter 3
Personality and Health

Once I got this crush on my teacher, Mr. Millerd. I used to think about him a lot. It got so I was always thinking of him. If I raised my hand and he didn't call on me, I was miserable. If he did call on me and I didn't know the answer, I was miserable. I couldn't even eat, and that's something, because I like to eat.

I began to want to be alone all the time, and in my house there's no place to be alone. Annie has all her junk in our bedroom and is always playing dolls. The only place I could be alone was the bathroom. I used to invent there stories about Mr. Millerd and act them out in front of the mirror. I do that a lot—make up stories, I mean. I can think of some pretty wild ones.

But with Mr. Millerd it was different. I never acted happy. I mean, no matter what I thought of, it was sad. I was always dying for him. . . .

from "Twice I Said I Love You," by Teresa Giardina in *Datebook Magazine*, Young World Press

Your endocrine and nervous systems work together to keep your body running smoothly. In order to keep "all systems go," your body has certain needs. You must keep up the maintenance of the systems of your body by getting enough sleep, a proper diet, and regular exercise.

How much sleep is "enough," and why is it needed? The amount of sleep needed is not the same for each person. If you wake up in the morning feeling exhausted, you are probably not getting enough sleep. On the other hand, getting too much sleep can have similar effects.

Why would a person get too much sleep? Some people sleep to avoid problems. Some people would rather sleep than face the kind of life that they lead when awake—because their lives are painful, boring, or troublesome. Worry and fear can make us feel tired, just as a normal day's work can. The difference is that after a normal day, sleep will make us feel better. But sleep will not solve the problems that made us worried and tired.

What is it that sleep does for us? Again, scientists are still learning about the human body. They don't know all there is to know about sleep. It seems clear that sleep is necessary to give the body a chance to slow down and clear away some of the waste products of the muscles and nerve cells. When you sleep, the functions of your body slow down, and the body gets a chance to clean itself up and rebuild some of the cells and tissues that were destroyed during the day.

Dreams are also an important part of sleep. Scientists have discovered that if a person is permitted to sleep each night, but prevented from dreaming, that person will quickly develop symptoms of mental illness.

Apparently, the brain is able to use dreams to cope with information it has received during the day. Many of our problems appear in our dreams. Psychologists have studied

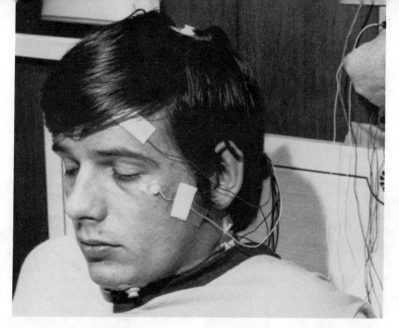

dreams for a long time as a way of understanding the problems of their patients. They have found that the language of dreams is *symbolic*. This means that the things we dream about stand for something else that we may know from everyday life. A man who dreams about a monster chasing him, for instance, may be worried about all the bills that are coming in. Or he may be afraid of his boss firing him.

Every person's dreams are his own, and a symbol that means one thing in one person's dream usually means something else in another's. People who sell books with explanations of what your dreams mean are often not qualified to analyze them correctly. A psychologist who knows you well is the kind of person who can tell you what your dream-symbols stand for.

Just as you need a balanced amount of sleep—not too much and not too little—you need a balanced diet. Some people eat three meals a day; others prefer four, five, or even more. What is important is that you eat the right kinds of food.

If you eat something each day from each of the *four essential food groups*, your diet will be basically healthy. The four groups include: 1) milk and dairy products, such as ice cream and cheese; 2) bread and cereal products; 3)

A Guide to Good Eating

Use Daily:

Milk Group

3 or more glasses milk — Children
smaller glasses for some children under 8

4 or more glasses — Teenagers

2 or more glasses — Adults

Cheese, ice cream and other milk-made foods can supply part of the milk

Meat Group

2 or more servings

Meats, fish, poultry, eggs, or cheese — with dry beans, peas, nuts as alternates

Vegetables and Fruits

4 or more servings

Include dark green or yellow vegetables; citrus fruit or tomatoes

Breads and Cereals

4 or more servings

Enriched or whole grain Added milk improves nutritional values

This is the foundation for a good diet. Use more of these and other foods as needed for growth, for activity, and for desirable weight.

The nutritional statements made in this leaflet have been reviewed by the Council on Foods and Nutrition of the American Medical Association and found consistent with current authoritative medical opinion.

meat products, including meat, poultry, shellfish, fish, eggs, peanut butter, dry beans, dry peas, lentils, and nuts; 4) vegetables and fruits.

A poor diet can affect both your endocrine and nervous systems. It can cause disease, personality problems, and retarded intellectual development.

On the other hand, your emotions can affect the way you eat. For example, perhaps a person starts to over-eat because he has difficulty dealing with people. Then, as he becomes overweight, the problem grows worse. The more he eats and the fatter he grows, the less able he is to meet people and make friends. Pretty soon he is eating even more because he feels bad, and to make up for not having friends. This is called *compensation*.

At other times, nervousness or excitement may cause you to lose your appetite. Even when this happens, you should try to eat something for nourishment and strength.

Many people leave the house in the morning after a breakfast of only a cup of coffee or a roll. Doctors advise against this practice because a good breakfast is necessary for energy and alertness throughout the day. About one-fourth of your daily requirement of food should be eaten at breakfast.

Whenever you eat, you should try to have a good atmosphere for your meal. Conversation should be pleasant. The dinner table is not the place to fight or argue. Anger and food do not mix. When you are angry, your stomach cannot digest food properly.

Finally, your body needs exercise. Exercise is not just for building muscles. Your body needs work every day just to maintain its level of strength. Lack of exercise can make you *lethargic* (very lazy and tired), prone to injury, and can bring on heart disease and other ailments.

You need exercise for psychological reasons also. How far can you run? How much weight can you lift? How many pushups can you do? It gives you a feeling of satisfaction to be able to do these things and meet new goals you set for yourself. Exercise and competitive sports are healthy ways to work off excess energy and aggressive feelings.

The type of exercise you do is up to you. The pleasure of competitive games such as tennis and basketball is well known. Some people prefer walking, riding bicycles, or swimming. Any type of exercise that you enjoy is generally fine for you.

Study Aids

I. *The Vocabulary of Psychology*

The three words and the phrase in the left column each belong with a phrase in the right column. In your notebook, write the number of the word or phrase at the left and match it with the letter of the phrase to which it belongs.

1. compensation

2. four essential
   food groups

3. symbolic

4. lethargic

a. the language of dreams
b. a feeling of laziness and lack of energy
c. a balanced diet needs something from each of these
d. doing something to make up for not having something else

II. *Understanding Personality and Health*

Some of the statements that follow are incorrect. Rewrite the sentences that are false to make them true. Do not simply insert words such as "not," "don't," "isn't," etc.

a. Exercise is needed mostly for building muscle strength.
b. The four basic food groups are fish, eggs, milk, and candy.
c. The language of dreams is composed of symbols.
d. Nervousness or excitement may cause you to lose your appetite.
e. Different people may need different amounts of sleep.
f. Worry and fear can make us feel tired.
g. Science has shown us the meaning of sleep.

64

h. Dreams help to resolve problems of real life.

i. Doctors say about one-fourth of your daily food requirement should be eaten at breakfast.

III. *Talking It Over*

1. Thomas Edison, the inventor of the light bulb and other products, claimed he only got four or five hours sleep a night. But he had a couch in his laboratory where he took short naps during the day. Would you prefer to sleep on this kind of schedule? What prevents you?

2. In many tropical countries, work stops around 11 o'clock in the morning and the people go home to sleep until the hottest part of the day is over. Then they go back to work. This is called a *siesta*. How would you like to sleep on this kind of schedule? Do you think it would improve your rest? Would the quality of your work improve?

3. Men originally slept at night because there was no artificial light except torches and candles, which were sometimes too smoky to use indoors. Today, with artificial light so bright and efficient, some people have suggested that we keep school buildings open all night long, and let those who prefer come to school at night instead of during the day. What do you think of this suggestion?

Unit III | Understanding Others

Chapter 1
Why Understand Others?

*. . . No man is an Iland, intire of it selfe; every man
is a peece of the Continent, a part of the maine;
if a Clod bee washed away by the Sea, Europe is
the lesse, as well as if a Promontorie were, as
well as if a Mannor of thy friends or of thine owne
were; any mans death diminishes me, because I
am involved in Mankinde; And therefore never
send to know for whom the bell tolls; It tolls for
thee . . .*

XVII Meditation, John Donne, 1571-1631

Adaptation
*. . . No man is an island by itself. Every man is a
piece of the continent, a part of the whole. If a
fistful of earth is washed away by the sea, Europe
is less, as well as if a cliff were, as well as if a
house of your friends or of your family were. Any
man's death makes me less, because I am a part
of mankind. And therefore never ask to know for
whom the bell tolls. It tolls for you.*

Did you ever know anybody who said people meant
nothing to him? Would you believe a person who said something like that? Would you think he was a very emotional
person?

Probably not, because our emotions are mostly
caused by what other people say and do. Emotions are our
reactions to other people, whether the emotions are love,
hate, fear, jealousy, like, dislike, or whatever. A person who
would have nothing to do with other people would have
no emotions, and a person with no emotions would be in bad
shape psychologically. Very likely, he would be mentally ill.

Because emotions are necessary, so is contact with other people. In fact, we meet dozens and dozens of people every day. Some of them may be good friends whom we know well. Some of them may be total strangers. All of them influence us in one way or another.

Most people like to get along well with other people. Most people want to have many acquaintances, some good friends, and a few people very close to them, whom they love and who love them. Most people do not like to have other people dislike them or be angry with them. Most people would rather not argue or fight or hurt other people's feelings. Why is it, then, that we so often have difficulty getting along with others?

At least part of the reason is that it is hard to understand why other people act the way they do. If we meet a friend of ours on the street and say hello, and he ignores us, we may get angry and think he's trying to put us down. In fact, he may be worrying about a problem at home and be so distracted that he didn't hear us say hello. If we knew about his problem at home, we might feel sorry for him, rather than angry.

Understanding why people behave the way they do is not easy. It is not even easy for us to understand why we behave the way we do. So it shouldn't be surprising that it is sometimes hard for us to understand other people. Still, it is possible to understand the other person's point of view. One of the reasons people argue and hurt each other's feelings is that they do not take the time to try to understand.

People are different. Not all people respond in the same way in different situations. What you think is a normal reaction may only be your reaction. It may not be someone else's.

For instance, in most American homes, it is normal for brothers and sisters to grow up together, showing affection for one another. Yet in the Sioux Indian tribes of old, brothers and sisters were not permitted to look at each other. They were kept separated until they were adults.

People who have grown up in different cultures will respond differently to a given situation.

This is an example of a difference between two *cultures*. A culture is the life-style of the place and time people live in. Sometimes there can be more than one culture in the same area. New York City, for example, has people in it who live in many different ways. Yet these differences are generally accepted so that the people of the city live, for the most part, in peace.

And differences in life-styles can exist within the same culture even within a single neighborhood, or within the same house. This does not mean that the people who live with each other have to be continually fighting. Just because a person likes different things than you do or lives differently, does not necessary mean that he dislikes your way of doing things, or that you have to dislike him.

When you do not understand the behavior of a friend or acquaintance, or of your parents, brothers, or sisters, try to imagine yourself in their place. Try to understand how you would act if you were the other person. If you still cannot understand the other person's behavior, then try to remember more exactly what his behavior was. Have you ever acted the same way? How were you feeling at the time? What might be the reason for this other person to be feeling that way now?

How can you put yourself in the other person's place? Isn't it better just to accept your own feelings and act on them? Not necessarily.

Take an example. Judy had been working on a project for a Halloween dance for the last three weeks. She designed a float and organized a committee to build it. The chairman of the Halloween dance was Bob. Judy thought Bob was the best-looking boy in the school. Two weeks ago he had told Judy he was glad she was designing the float and he asked her to have a Coke with him. Judy had a good time, and thought Bob seemed to, as well.

On the day Judy showed the class the completed float, everybody congratulated her. They all said she had done a great job. On her way home, she was happy and excited. Suddenly she ran into Bob outside the school building. He just mumbled, "Hi," and walked away very quickly.

Judy was hurt and upset.

What should she have done?

She might have decided that Bob was stuck-up and that she would never speak to him again. She could have gone and cried in her room. She could have told all her friends what a snob he was and how sorry she was for having anything to do with him or the dance. She could have tried to get them all on her side. She could have tried to get to know one of Bob's close friends and told him how rotten she thought Bob was.

Some of these things sound silly when we see them on paper. This is because we don't know Bob and Judy very well. They are only figures in a book. But when disappointing things like this actually happen to us, many people react in ways just like the ones suggested above.

A better reaction for Judy would be for her to put herself in Bob's place. She knew he must have liked her, since he obviously had a good time on their date. He probably kept on liking her, but was too busy with the dance to ask her out again. If that was the case, he might have been embarrassed when he met her. He might have thought she would be angry with him because he hadn't asked her out again. Very often, adolescent boys are most ill at ease with girls they like very much.

If that was the case, none of the ways Judy can "get back" at him to show she is hurt and angry will do much good. She should continue to be friendly to Bob, and show him that she wasn't upset because he didn't have time to ask her out again.

Understanding others helps you to get along. You make things easier for yourself when you try to understand what others mean. You can also make things easier by trying to let other people know just how *you* feel. This does not mean that you should throw a temper tantrum when someone makes you angry. It means that you should not try to pretend that you feel one way when you feel another. You should be honest with yourself and others.

Study Aids

I. *The Vocabulary of Psychology*

In the left-hand column below are two words. Copy these in your notebook and next to each one, write the numbers of the definitions on the right that correctly belong with each.

a. emotions   1. differences in behavior in different countries may be caused by this

b. culture   2. necessary for mental health

3. our reactions to other people

4. the life-style of a people of a certain time and place

5. love, hate, and fear are some

6. different areas of the same city may be different in this way

7. it is not good to hide them

II. *Understanding Others*

Some of the statements that follow are incorrect Rewrite the sentences that are false to make them true. Do not simply insert words such as "not," "don't," "isn't," etc.

1. To be mentally healthy, a person should not have strong emotions.

2. Most people like to get along well with other people.

3. When you don't understand someone else's behavior, you should try to imagine yourself in his place.

4. People respond in different ways to different situations.

5. A culture is the life-style of the time and place people live in.
6. It is not easy to understand why people talk and act the way they do.
7. If you don't understand someone, you should avoid him to save yourself trouble.

III. *Talking It Over*

1. Barbara liked Raul very much, and would save a place in the lunchroom for him everyday so they could eat together. One day he didn't show up, and she didn't see him. Later that afternoon, one of Barbara's friends told her that Raul ate lunch outside of school with some other girl. When she saw Raul later, Barbara walked away and wouldn't speak to him. What do you think she should have done? Why?

2. Bonnie was president of her class. Her teacher, Mr. Roma, promised that he would take the class to the museum downtown one afternoon. Most of the class was looking forward to the trip. Two days before they were scheduled to go, a box of slides was reported missing from the art room after Bonnie's class had been there. Mr. Roma announced that the trip to the museum would be called off unless the slides were returned. The day before the trip, the slides were missing and some of the class asked Bonnie to speak to Mr. Roma. What would you say to him if you were her?

3. Joe was serious about photography, and so was Mr. Halsey, the school's audio-visual director. Joe spent most of his free periods helping out—handling the projectors, showing slides and running the tape recorders. Mr. Halsey had given him some good advice about developing and printing photographs. One day Joe brought some photographs to show Mr. Halsey. Mr. Halsey didn't really look at them, and he said,

"Listen, Joe, why don't you work harder in shop—try being a carpenter or something!"

Do you think Mr. Halsey said what he did because Joe's photographs weren't any good—or because Mr. Halsey was upset about something else?

Chapter 2
Thinking Clearly About Other People

Thoughts While Driving Home

Was I clever enough? Was I charming?
Did I make at least one good pun?
Was I disconcerting? Disarming?
Was I wise? Was I wan? Was I fun?

Did I answer that girl with white shoulders
Correctly, or should I have said
(Engagingly), "Kierkegaard smolders,
But Eliot's ashes are dead"?

And did I, while being a smarty,
Yet some wry reserve slyly keep,
So they murmured, when I'd left the party,
"He's deep. He's deep. He's deep"?

by John Updike, from *Telephone Poles and Other Poems,* (NY: Alfred A. Knopf, Inc., 1959)

As your body matures, so does your personality. One sign of a mature personality is the ability to think clearly about other people. A mature person sees other people as people like himself. They have needs and emotions similar to his own. A mature person sees that respect for the feelings of others is necessary if he wants to have his own feelings respected.

Mature people learn that words like "hip," "sharp," "cool," and "a drag" are not as useful as more precise and real descriptions. For example, Joan had a date with Fred, a boy in her school. Afterwards, she described him to all her friends as "a real drag." Since Joan was a popular girl in her school, her opinion carried. The other girls started to giggle

whenever they saw Fred. Soon, there wasn't a girl in the school who would go out with him.

What really happened on their date was this. Joan had hoped to be asked out that night by Charles, a "groovy" guy who Joan thought was really "with it." When Charles didn't ask her out, Joan accepted a date with Fred. Even if Charles had called later, Joan would have broken the date with Fred.

Joan was angry with herself for having to accept a date with Fred. He didn't fit in with the way she thought of herself. He was a quiet boy who didn't dress the way her friends did. Joan expected him to take her to a nice place and spend a lot of money. She figured she was worth it.

She was in a bad mood when Fred arrived. When he said that he was short of money and that he thought they could just take a walk downtown and look at store windows and have a hamburger, Joan got really furious. She hardly said a word all evening.

Do you think that Fred should have spent the evening trying to coax Joan to be pleasant? Do you think that Fred deserved the treatment Joan gave him? Fred probably had no opportunity or desire to be entertaining after Joan's rude treatment.

Suppose that Joan had described what really happened to her friends. What might she have said? She could have admitted that Fred was a quiet, thoughtful person. She could have added that she herself preferred to spend time with someone more lively but that one of her friends might like Fred.

In other words, Joan could hardly have changed her feelings much with regard to Fred, but she could have avoided putting him down to her friends. She might have easily done a little clear thinking about Fred's good qualities. She didn't behave in a mature way.

What about the opposite situation? What happens when you have a friend that you call "hip" or "groovy," or some other word that suggests that you think he or she is great? Do you ever stop to analyze the reasons why they are great? Or if they really are?

Take the case of Len and John. Len always described John as a great guy. He never bothered to analyze, or figure out, just what his friend's good qualities were. Why did he like John? Well, because John was just "good old John." They had been friends for as long as Len could remember.

Then, one summer vacation, Len went away and when he came back John had made some new friends. And he seemed different, although Len couldn't explain it to himself—not until the party. A lot of the kids at the party were "high" on something. And John pulled out two marijuana cigarettes.

"Here, have a stick, Len—get with it." John even bragged that he had tried Heroin. "It was real cool, Len."

What should Len do? Go along with John? Refuse to have anything more to do with John? What he could have done was to think clearly about what John's good qualities were. Then maybe he could have helped John to understand his own strengths and solve his problems in a better way.

During adolescence, you spend a lot of time with your friends. It is important for you to be accepted by a group. Most teen-agers are not yet mature enough to stand on their own. At the same time, it is important to begin the process of maturing by learning to think clearly about other people. Although you need to win your friends' approval, you shouldn't make blind judgments about who are friends and who are not. You shut out a vital part of your experience by shutting out people who are new or different.

One of the ways in which you can learn to think clearly about other kinds of people is by making an effort to get to know them. This can be very pleasant. For instance, if you live in a large city, you can visit some sections where people of different *nationalities* and cultures live. This means people who came, or whose parents or grandparents came, from different countries. Many large cities have a China-town section, where people of Chinese ancestry live. There you can eat Chinese food and shop in stores that sell Chinese goods. You can get to know the food and the customs of people different from the group from which you come, and perhaps even some words of a different language. Many *ethnic* or national groups live in areas like this. Italian, Latin American, Jewish, Afro-American, Greek, German, and many other kinds of peoples have their own restaurants and shops that represent their culture.

You will learn by meeting many kinds of people that all people are interesting. We tend to think of groups of people as being all alike. Yet members of a group are individuals, as you will find out when you meet some of them. Each member of a group is an individual, but they all contribute to the group culture.

A person who shuts out different peoples or groups from his circle of friends becomes narrow-minded. He or she is missing many experiences that contribute to the development of a mature personality. A great deal of energy that should be spent enjoying the world is wasted. At this time in your life, you should be open to all kinds and groups of people. The more people you meet, the better you will be able to understand and think clearly about them.

Study
Aids

I. *Understanding Other People*

Some of the statements that follow are incorrect. Rewrite the sentences that are false to make them true. Do not simply insert words such as "not," "don't," "isn't," etc.

1. It is important during adolescence for people to belong to groups.
2. The more mature your personality is, the better able you are to think clearly about other people.
3. Joan acted immaturely on her date with Fred.
4. It pays to be cautious around people you don't know.
5. A nationality is a group of people who came from a certain country, or whose ancestors came from that country.
6. If we think about our friends' good qualities, we can better judge how they are likely to react to unexpected situations.

II. *Talking It Over*

1. Do you have an idea about the sort of person that might hold a certain job? What sort of person, for instance, might be a truck driver? An accountant? A policeman? A pro football player? A used car salesman? Thinking that each of these must be a certain kind of person is called thinking in *stereotypes*. Thinking in stereotypes means thinking that all members of a group are alike. Racial stereotypes result in racial prejudice, but, as you can see, you might have stereotyped thoughts about other kinds of groups as well. Is it a good idea to think this way? Why do people think in stereotypes at all? Give some other examples of stereotyped thinking.

2. Ellen's boyfriend Robert had very long hair. The teachers at school were always telling him he ought to cut it. One day, a substitute teacher began teasing him about his hair in the lunchroom. The substitute teacher tried to put a flower in his hair. Robert got angry and shoved her, and she fell backwards over a chair. He was suspended from school. When Ellen's parents heard about this, they told her she couldn't go out with him anymore. If you were Ellen, how would you explain Robert's conduct to your parents? What do you think the parents might say?

3. Felipe's friend Geraldo was fun to be with. He was always playing jokes on other people. He tied people's shoes together in class. He put ice cubes down the backs of girls' blouses. He put salt in the sugar containers at lunch. One of his favorite tricks was to break the locks on people's lockers so they couldn't get into them.

One Friday night, Felipe and Geraldo went out with two girls they knew, Kate and Teresa. Felipe really liked Teresa and wanted to impress her. However, at a restaurant they went to, Geraldo put some ice cream on Teresa's chair, and when she sat down it got all over her dress. She got angry and both the girls left. Geraldo said it just showed they didn't have a sense of humor.

What would you say to Geraldo if you were Felipe? What would Felipe think if he took the time to think clearly about Geraldo?

Chapter 3
Guides to Social Behavior

Lady Bracknell:
> *Pardon me, you are not engaged to anyone.*
> *When you do become engaged to someone, I*
> *or your father, should his health permit him,*
> *will inform you of the fact. An engagement should*
> *come on a young girl as a surprise, pleasant or*
> *unpleasant, as the case may be. It is hardly a*
> *matter she could be allowed to arrange for herself...*
> *And now I have a few questions to put to you,*
> *Mr. Worthington. While I am making these*
> *inquiries, you, Gwendolen, will wait for me below*
> *in the carriage.*

from *The Importance of Being Earnest*, by Oscar Wilde (Act 1. Scene 1)

People get together in what we call *social situations*. Social is a word meaning "having to do with other people." A social situation is an activity where two or more people are gathered together. How most people behave in a social situation is partly a matter of how they feel and partly a matter of certain rules or guides for conduct.

Most people grow up learning a certain way to act. People from different societies learn different ways of acting. Among the kind of people they grow up with, their particular way of acting is called good manners.

In all societies, good manners make life easier. In crowded cities, it's hard to get along without them. Having good manners means more than the simple rules for conduct that say you should eat with your napkin in your lap. Good manners means consideration and respect for other people.

In our society, a considerate person does not shove people out of line in supermarkets or push in front of them in the cafeteria. Having good manners means you introduce a friend when you meet people he doesn't know. Good manners means that you try to talk about the good points of your friends rather than gossiping about their failures. It means that you don't disturb people who are working or studying by talking loudly, screaming, or shouting. If you are considerate of other people, you will find that basic good manners will come to you automatically.

Have you ever been standing with a teacher, a friend's father or mother, or some other adult when suddenly a friend of yours appeared and stood awkwardly beside you, waiting to be introduced? Perhaps at such a time you wished that you could remember the rules for introductions. These rules are very easy to remember, especially if you practice making introductions to fit certain situations.

Which person do you introduce first? Simply say first the name of the person you wish to "favor" or show respect for: a woman before a man, and an older person before a younger person. For example: *"Mother*, this is my

friend from school, Jennifer Wilson. Jennifer, this is my mother." Or if you are walking down the street with your teacher and you meet Mr. Johnson, an older man: "*Mr. Johnson*, I'd like you to meet my teacher, Mr. Cardwell, Mr. Cardwell, this is Mr. Johnson."

When there is no one to introduce you to a new person, you might try risking the first friendly move. It is perfectly acceptable for either a boy or a girl to say hello to a member of the opposite sex, even if they have never been introduced. This is especially true if the person who is greeted is seen frequently at school, church, etc.

When you're out with friends or on a date, you should try to be aware of other people's likes and dislikes. Some of your friends may like to go to movies. Some of your other friends may prefer to go to a basketball game or watch ice hockey on television. Some people enjoy talking about good books or classical music. Others are interested in rock music or jazz. In general, people will enjoy your company more if you are able to identify their interests and wishes and adapt your own behavior to those differences.

For instance, if John has never read a book that was not required reading for school, perhaps it is not considerate of you to spend forty-five minutes with him describing the latest book you have read. On the other hand, if Sue has always enjoyed ice skating, but never seen ice hockey played, it would show your awareness of her interests to ask her to go with you the next time you have two tickets to an ice hockey game.

The "rules of dating" are something that many teen-agers feel concerned about. Boys worry that if they do not behave properly girls will be offended or laugh at them. Girls worry about what to say and do on a date.

These worries are natural. On a date, as in any social situation, the "rule" is to be as friendly and courteous as possible. Your good intentions will show, and your date will respond in a friendly manner.

When calling a girl to ask for a date, the boy should state some specific activity he has in mind. "Would you like to go to the basketball game on Friday night?" He should not ask, "Doing anything Friday night?"

If the girl has to ask her parents whether she can go and what time she has to be home, the boy should not be offended. On the other hand, the girl should not try to put the boy off, hoping that someone else will call her. This is very rude and inconsiderate. She should give him an answer immediately and should try to make a refusal as polite as possible.

Many young teen-agers are not ready for relationships with the opposite sex. Boys and girls should not feel pressured to start dating at an earlier age than they really want to. You will have plenty of time to catch up, no matter how late you start.

Meeting together in groups is a good way to start dating. When a boy is ready to "single date," he will naturally ask one of the girls from the group for a date. He will feel more at ease if he has already had practice in talking to and being with girls in groups.

It is important to practice social relationships. One reason boys and girls sometimes feel uneasy in each other's company is that they have not had enough practice in being with the other sex. This practice comes naturally in school, and activities that are planned for after school.

It has been traditional for a boy to pay all the expenses of a date. This is still true on more formal dates, but it has become quite acceptable for couples to share expenses on less formal occasions. You can be sure that whatever you decide to do, you will not be the only ones doing it.

There are advantages to a girl paying her own way. She gets to have more say in what she and her date will do, and she doesn't have to feel obligated to him. He in turn will know that she is spending time with him because she wants to be with him and not because of his money or status.

Most manners are only standardized ways of being thoughtful to others. For instance, manners in a restaurant are the same as manners at your own dinner table. In a restaurant, however, there is service, and you should be courteous to those who serve you. That is just a matter of being pleasant and thoughtful of others' feelings! Then, in a restaurant, the girl is supposed to walk ahead of the boy to the table. Her chair is pulled out for her by her escort, or by the waiter. That's considered polite, too. But it comes from a time when girls were thought of as too fragile to lift anything as heavy as a chair for themselves! And it is still considered correct, in formal restaurants, for the girl to give her order to her escort, who then gives the waiter both their orders. It is easier for the waiter that way, and so the custom continues. But in the past the reason for this was that a young lady was not supposed to speak to a waiter herself.

At the table, forks, knives, and spoons are used from the outside inward, as each course is served. Thus, the soup spoon is on the outside, then the coffee or dessert spoon. The salad fork is outside the dinner fork. Utensils (knives, forks, and spoons) are left on the plate after use. Glasses are used from right to left, if there is more than one glass. Wine glasses are to the right of water glasses.

In the home, manners are just as important as on outside social occasions. You should get practice in using good manners at home so that they will seem familiar to you when you go out. Young people should show courtesy to older people. When a guest comes to your home, you should take his or her coat and offer a chair. Being friendly and courteous at all times is impressive to people. It will make you feel good about yourself and your manners.

When travelling to strange neighborhoods and foreign countries, manners are especially important. When others do not understand our language and customs, good manners often act as a bridge between different cultures. Whether or not you are familiar with the local customs of a certain place, your basic friendliness and courtesy will always make your intentions known.

Study Aids

Understanding Guides to Social Behavior

On your paper, write the letter of the phrase that shows the best manners.

1. To introduce your friend Ralph to your Uncle George.
   a. "Ralph, this is my Uncle George."
   b. "Uncle George, I'd like you to meet Ralph. Ralph, this is my Uncle George."
   c. "Here's my Uncle George, Ralph. Uncle George, this is Ralph."

2. To ask Carolyn, the girl next door whom you go out with often, to see a movie on Friday. (You are a boy.)
   a. "What are you doing Friday night, Carolyn?"
   b. "Did you see the picture that's at the Paramount?"
   c. "I was wondering if you'd like to go see a movie on Friday. There's a good one at the Paramount."

3. To reply to Bob, the boy next door who is a friend but not the most exciting guy in the world, who has asked you to a movie on Friday night. (You are a girl.)
   a. "I'll let you know Thursday night, O.K., Bob?"
   b. "Couldn't we go roller skating instead?"
   c. "I'll have to ask my mother if I can go."

4. To ask Perry, an attractive boy in your class who has been friendly to you but hasn't asked you out, if he wants to come to a small party on Saturday at your house. (You are a girl.)
   a. "Some of the kids from school are bringing their records over Saturday, Perry. I'm going

to make some pizza. Would you like to come, about 7:30?"

b. "I'm having some people over Saturday, Perry. If you want to come, you can."

c. "Joe's bringing Ann and Jack's bringing Barbara over to my house Saturday night, Perry. I'd like you to come as my guest. How about it?"

II. Talking It Over

1. Janelle's father worked nights, and slept at home during part of the day. If you have this situation at home, you know it caused problems for Janelle and her family. She liked to have her friends in after school, and they all liked to play records loudly.

Finally, her father said that his rest was more important than Janelle's fun and that she couldn't bring any of her friends home in the afternoon. Janelle shouted that she would be too ashamed to go to anybody else's house if she couldn't have them into her own home. Can you suggest some ways of solving this problem?

2. Roy wanted to impress Ruth, so he took her to a fancy restaurant. The menu was printed in French and Roy had to ask the waiter for help. He felt as if the waiter was making fun of him and was very embarrassed. Ruth knew he was embarrassed, but could see the waiter was only trying to help. Can good manners help you in a situation like this? Explain how.

3. On another occasion, Randy took Dorothy to a small Italian restaurant. The waiter seemed very rude, brought the whole meal at once, and took the dishes away before they were finished. He was trying to rush them because people were waiting for tables. Randy was irritated, and didn't leave any tip. The waiter saw this and got very angry. He followed them to the door shouting that he depended on tips for his living. Do you think Randy was right not to leave a tip? What would you have done?

Chapter 4
Making Friends

Bill and Ray liked each other. They had known one another for years and spent much of their time together. Often they got into Bill's car and went driving through their home town. Bill was always whistling at every attractive girl who walked by. In fact, when Bill wasn't whistling at girls, he was talking about them. He always gave Ray the impression that he was an expert on girls. But somehow Ray knew something: No matter how much Bill whistled and talked about girls, he was scared stiff of them.

You probably have a number of friends already. But you may have become friends with them because you lived in the same neighborhood. Or your parents might have been friends with their parents. Now you go to school with people from different neighborhoods and different backgrounds. You have found that you are beginning to make your own choices about friends.

What should you look for in a friend?

A friend is someone who is good for you to know. A friend thinks of your feelings and your needs. Someone once said, "A friend is someone who still likes you, even though he knows all about you." Do you think this statement is true?

A real friend will try to help you out, even though he has to go to some expense or trouble to do so. For example, Saul was home from school with the flu for a week. Gene had a book that Saul needed to keep up with his homework, but they lived far apart. Still, Gene took the bus to Saul's house to bring him the book. Did Gene act like a friend?

How can you meet people who will become your friends? There are many ways. At this stage in life, by just being friendly to people you meet, you will naturally make friends. You can meet people easily by doing activities and by joining clubs that interest you. That way, you will meet others with similar interests. Then you may want to invite them to your home.

Sometimes people become friends even though they have different interests. Judy liked to sew. She made all her own clothes and could talk for hours about patterns and fabrics. Grace, on the other hand, was interested in sports. She made the tennis team. Grace and Judy were good friends, despite their different interests. Grace complimented Judy on her clothes and even learned a little sewing from her. Judy came to matches to watch Grace play tennis. Neither was bored by the other's interests. In fact, they admired each other for their different accomplishments.

What makes a friend? It is not always a person with the same interests, but having the same interests helps. What is necessary is a mutual respect and trust. When you know you can really count on someone, that person is a friend.

There are bad relationships as well as good ones. A relationship in which one of the friends depends too much on the other is bad for both. For instance, Hal had a friend, Fred. Fred was always telling people that Hal was his best friend. He would call Hal up and tell him all his troubles. He would whine and complain. He was always asking for advice and help. He couldn't even do his school assignments without first calling Hal and asking him how to do them. All his spare time was spent with Hal. But in a real emergency, Hal could never count on Fred.

Fred was behaving immaturely in this relationship. He was not being a good friend to Hal. Hal was the mature one, and Fred was more like his son than his friend. But by letting Fred hang around all the time, Hal was keeping him from finding real friends and having to stand on his own.

In some friendships, one person will try to drag the other down to his level. Drug addicts look for friends they can "turn on." A person who turns someone else on to hard drugs is not a friend—he is an enemy. If you have a friend who makes you feel that you have to do what he does to stay friends with him, remember that a friendship is two-sided.

There are other people in the world and you can make other friends.

A mature person can, but does not try to, live without friends. If he finds that he is leaving his present friends behind in moving on to new and different interests, he looks for other friends.

It cannot be too heavily stressed how important it is for the development of personality to meet as many new people as possible. You can and should meet and make friends with people of all ages, backgrounds, and races.

Older people have many experiences to share. Naturally, however, most of your friends will be your own age. You will want to dress and act pretty much as others of your age and group dress and act. But if you spend too much of your energy in keeping up with the crowd, you will pay a price in later development. If there are people that you keep out of your circle of friends because of a prejudice against the way they dress, look, or act, you are becoming narrow-minded instead of mature. A narrow-minded person does not have the type of personality that can really enjoy life.

Study Aids

I. *Understanding Making Friends*

Some of the statements that follow are incorrect. Rewrite the sentences that are false to make them true. Do not simply insert words such as "not," "don't," "isn't," etc.

  a. A friend is someone who is good for you to know.
  b. People with different interests cannot be friends.
  c. Mature people do not try to live without friends.
  d. We cannot have any friends who are younger or older than we are.
  e. Meeting new people keeps one's personality from developing.
  f. We should try to hold on to our friends, no matter how much they change.

II. *Talking It Over*

1. Are your good friends now the same people that were your good friends five years ago? What about the friends you used to have? What happened to them? Why do you have different friends now? Why did the old friends stop being so close to you? Was it your decision, theirs, or a combination? Did either of you make a conscious decision to stop being friends? If your friends today are the same people that were your friends five years ago, can you think of any ways in which your personalities changed together? What are they?

2. Why do you think most people have friends of around their own age? Is this true of most of *your* friends? Would older or younger friends be any different, other than

94

in age, from the friends that are the same age as you? How might they be different? Would such differences contribute to your friendship or harm it? Explain.

3. There are many people, young and old, who are lonely because they cannot find others who share the same interests. What are some ways to find other people who are like yourself? Don't forget that meeting large numbers of people is not so easy for people who are not in school. Also, people may find that their classmates have different interests. People as different as Albert Einstein, John Lennon, Kareem Abdul-Jabbar were in schools where they felt separated from most of the other people. How can you become friends with people who are different from you?

Unit IV | Family Living

Chapter 1
Your Parents Are People

My father was a justice of the peace, and I
supposed he possessed the power of life and death
over all men, and could hang anybody that offended
him. This was distinction enough for me as a
general thing; but the desire to be a steamboatman
kept intruding, nevertheless. . . Boy after boy
managed to get on the river. The minister's son
became an engineer. The doctor and the post-
master's sons became "mud clerks"; the wholesale
liquor dealer's son became a barkeeper on a boat;
four sons of the chief merchant and two sons of the
county judge became pilots. . . Now some of us
were left disconsolate. We could not get on the
river—at least our parents would not let us.

So, by and by, I ran away. I said I would
never come home again till I was a pilot and could
come in glory. But somehow I could not manage it.

From *Life on the Mississippi,* by Mark Twain

Most children have grown up living with one or both
of their parents. You are so used to seeing your parents every
day that it is difficult for you to think of them *objectively.*
What does that mean: *objectively?* It means to think about
them as if they meant no more to you than anybody else.
When we meet someone new, we can think about them
objectively, watching what they do and say. We gradually
build up some idea of what they're like.

But it's hard to know what your parents are like. It's
hard to see them as just people. Why is that? Because we

are too *close* to them. When you think of your mother, you remember all the feelings, good and bad, that you have toward her. When you think of your father, you may think of the time he took you to a football game or the time he slapped you for coming in late. You might be thinking about a gift you want him to give you for your birthday or maybe an argument you had with him last week.

Much of the way you feel about your parents is related to the fact that they have brought you up. Probably they formed the way you think. Sometimes they laid down strict rules and regulations that were hard for you to follow. It is difficult for you to think of them without feeling close and loving, or angry and hurt—or perhaps a mixture of both kinds of feelings.

These feelings stop you from seeing your parents as they really are—as people, just like everybody else. They have their own needs which you may not appreciate. They have problems. They make mistakes. They don't always get their own way. They get tired. They think, sometimes, that people treat them unfairly. There are a lot of things they'd like to do but they can't. In short, your parents are people!

But it's hard for you to see that because you are used to thinking of your parents only in relation to yourself. If you realized that your parents are people, it would help you to understand the way they act.

Parents tend to forget that you are almost grown up. They sometimes think of you as a child, not as a young adult. They probably tell you that you are not mature enough to accept responsibility for your own actions, and you probably feel that they don't give you enough independence or responsibility.

Perhaps your parents hate to see you grow up and leave home. Perhaps they remember how little experience and understanding they had at your age. They remember the many mistakes they made. They want to keep you from making the same mistakes.

But you want to try things on your own, to be free to make your own mistakes. Now that you are older, you see that your parents continue to make mistakes. They may have habits that irritate you or attitudes and ways of thinking that you think they should change.

Your parents may often criticize you unfairly. Almost everyone's parents do this. They seem to expect you to be perfect, although they are far from perfect themselves. This may be a mistake your parents are making. How can you deal with it?

Jerry's mother was always telling him how clumsy he was. Every time he spilled his milk as a baby, she would yell at him. When he got older, he became less clumsy. But his mother always seemed to think of him as a clumsy baby.

One day he was helping her by sweeping the kitchen. He accidentally hit a leg of the kitchen table. The table buckled and several bottles of oil, vinegar, and juice that were standing on the table fell to the floor and were broken. As Jerry was cleaning up the mess, his mother came in and saw what he had done. "You're as clumsy as ever," she said. Jerry felt that his mother would never think he could do anything right. He stormed out of the house.

Jerry's mother was not right to criticize him in this instance. He had been trying to help her by sweeping the kitchen. He accidentally spilled the bottles. But Jerry's mother had just come in from a long, tiring day at work. She was looking forward to cooking supper for the family in a clean kitchen. Now she knew that time would be wasted cleaning up the mess.

Jerry didn't try to put himself in her place, either. He might have tried to understand the way she was feeling. He could have said, "I'm sorry I spilled those things. I know how tired you are. I'll clean it up and help with dinner." His mother might have realized then that he did not mean to do it and would probably have said so.

You need to explore and learn at this stage of your life. New interests should be claiming your energy and attention. Your parents make it possible for you to engage in these new activities. They are the ones who provide the home from which you go out to discover the world. A lot of their energy is taken up by providing the home. This tends to make them tired and irritable. By understanding this, the teen-ager can spare himself a lot of grief.

Are your parents too strict? Do they make what you think are unreasonable rules about what time you should be home at night? They are concerned about you.

If all your friends are allowed to come in at a certain hour, and you have to be in much earlier, you should discuss this with your parents. They can explain why they set a certain hour, and they may change their minds if you can discuss the matter calmly. All of you can understand each other better. You still may not agree, but understanding can do away with hard feelings.

Some children are forced to bring themselves up. Their parents are either absent from the home or too busy or ill to pay much attention to their children. For instance, Jean would come home from school every day to find her mother drunk. She had to take care of her younger brothers and sisters. She had no father. Jean often felt that she had no one to turn to. She wanted to drop out of school. She didn't know how to plan proper meals for her brothers and sisters. She was afraid that her mother would spend the housekeeping money on liquor.

What do you think Jean should do?

There are a number of ways you can get help if your parents are not responsible people. You might talk the problem over with some other relative: an uncle, aunt, or grandparent. You could see your school guidance counselor, or your minister or priest. There are also groups of teen-agers who meet and discuss their problems. One such group is Alateen, for the children of alcoholic parents.

Another common problem is divorce. When parents decide to get divorced, their children sometimes feel a deep sense of shame. Children can sometimes feel guilty about their parents getting divorced. They think if they had been better behaved, maybe father or mother wouldn't have left. These feelings of anxiety are natural, but not justified. Help is often needed in dealing with them before they get out of hand.

Children sometimes blame one or the other of their parents for the divorce. This is a mistake, usually. The problems that led up to the divorce were probably contributed by both parents, even though it may be easier to see one side of the problem.

Deep down, children have some good feelings for both parents. It is unfortunate if, after a divorce, they do not get to see the parent who lives outside the home.

Often, the remarriage of a parent means that family life gets started again in an improved way. Children sometimes resent their mother or father for remarrying, but everyone is likely to be better off if the parent is happier by remarrying.

There are other problems that can bring tension and unhappiness. One or both parents may become seriously ill,

and have to stay at home. In this case, it is a good idea to find out just what is wrong. Knowing this can help you to be sympathetic and understand the problems that must be faced. Talk about the problem to the parent who is well, or

102

to the doctor that treats the sick parent. Be honest with them about your own feelings, even if you are resentful or hurt.

The death of a parent when the children of the family are not yet grown can cause problems. Again, it is unwise to keep your feelings bottled up inside you if this should happen. Talk to your other parent. You will see that they too have been affected. The members of the family have to make a lot of adjustments. Talk with others who may have had the same experience.

Children may feel somehow responsible for their parent's death. They think that if they had been less trouble, perhaps their mother or father wouldn't have died. These feelings are wrong. Your parent is a separate human being from you. You have no control over how they are going to feel, or how they will react to something you did. Your own life will continue, and you should live it free from guilt or doubts. This is the best thing you can do for your parent.

Some children are raised in foster homes, or must live for long periods with other relatives. They may get the feeling that they are not loved as they would be by their real parents. This may not be true. Parents are not the only people who can feel love for you. Foster parents, or an uncle or aunt, can feel just as much love as your actual parents. Of course, nobody is pleasant all the time; real parents and substitute parents both make mistakes in raising children. None of the mistakes they make, or the bad moods they may get into, mean they don't love you. Learn to look beneath the surface. The reason they have you in their home in the first place is that they love you, and they enjoy raising children.

Some foster parents may receive money from the state government to pay for the child's clothes and medical expenses. Otherwise, they would not be able to afford to "work" at the "job" of raising children. Foster parents in some other countries are paid a salary in addition to expenses. Do you think there is much "work" to being a parent?

Study Aids

I. *Understanding Your Parents As People*

Some of the statements that follow are incorrect. Rewrite the sentences that are false to make them true. Do not simply insert words such as "not,", "don't," "isn't," etc.

a. Your feelings about your parents depend in part on the way they have brought you up.

b. It is easy for you to see your parents the way they really are.

c. Your parents' criticism of you may not always be fair.

d. It is necessary for you to explore and learn.

e. Talking things over with your parents is almost never helpful.

f. It is wise to put the blame on one parent for causing a divorce.

g. Foster parents make fewer mistakes than "real" parents in raising children.

II. *Talking It Over*

1. Lucy and Joey's mother was a nervous type. She was always screaming, "You kids will be the death of me," and "I can't stand this noise. You're killing me." One day she collapsed from nervous exhaustion and had to go away for a rest. Lucy and Joey felt that their mother's illness was their fault. They felt guilty. What advice would you give them?

2. Martha's parents were divorced and she lived with her mother. Her father was supposed to come and see her every other Sunday. Sometimes he would show up, but other

104

times he wouldn't. One Sunday, he promised to take Martha and her friend Janet to a play. They waited all day, and he didn't show up or call to say he wasn't coming. Martha was terribly embarrassed and ashamed. If you were Martha, what would you have said to Janet? What should Martha say to her father the next time she sees him? What should she do the next time he promises to meet her?

3. Jerry and his friends went to a drive-in movie that lasted later than he had told his parents it would. His friends decided after the movie that they would look for something to eat, and drove all over looking for a place that was still open. Jerry finally got home between 3 and 3:30 in the morning, and his parents were so angry they grounded him for a month. Jerry felt this was unfair, since he hadn't been doing the driving, and hadn't been in any trouble. If you were Jerry, how would you try to persuade your parents to lighten the punishment? How do you think Jerry's parents would respond to this argument? How should they respond?

Chapter 2
Living with Your Brothers and Sisters

THE QUARREL

I quarreled with my brother,
I don't know what about,
One thing led to another
And somehow we fell out.
The start of it was slight,
The end of it was strong,
He said he was right,
I knew he was wrong!

We hated one another.
The afternoon turned black.
Then suddenly my brother
Thumped me on the back,
And said, "Oh, come along!
We can't go on all night—
I was in the wrong."
So he was in the right.

by Eleanor Farjeon, from *Poems for Children* Lippincott, 1933

Some people have many brothers and sisters. Some don't have any. Some live in families of all boys or all girls. Others have one brother or one sister. Each kind of family has its own special advantages and special problems.

If you are an only child, you get more of your parents' time and they may have more money to spend on you. But you miss the companionship and fun of having brothers and sisters.

On the other hand, if your family is a large one, you will have plenty of companionship. But you may sometimes wish you had more privacy.

Suppose that you are a girl who has an older sister 18 years old and a brother 11 years old. You are about halfway between them in age. Perhaps you think your older sister sometimes treats you badly. When she brings her friends home and you are interested in what they are doing, they push you out of the room and lock the door. Even though you are very curious about what they are doing, you should respect their privacy. At some other time you may want privacy, and your sister will be more apt to respect your wishes. In many ways, she may be pleasant to have as a sister. She may lend you a sweater or show you a new way to fix your hair or pay the fine on your library book. It's hard for you to understand how she really feels about you.

How does your little brother behave? He probably wants to follow you wherever you go. He wants to hang around with your friends. If you think carefully, you will realize that you probably treat your little brother the same way your older sister treats you.

Brothers and sisters in most families have some arguments. But there are many advantages in having brothers and sisters. If you are older than they are, they don't have to be a bother. Probably they look up to you, even if they don't always show it. If they are very young, you can have good times taking them places and teaching them new things.

If your brothers and sisters are older than you, they will have their own friends and interests that they may not always want to share with you. Be patient, and remember that there are times when you want to be alone with your own friends. You have a good chance to learn about the problems and pleasures of growing up by having an older brother or sister.

There is always competition between brothers and sisters. The name for this competition is *sibling rivalry*. A sibling is your brother or sister. Often brothers and sisters compete for attention or special privileges from their

parents. Sometimes the parents aggravate this rivalry. Parents say, "Why can't you be polite like your sister?" or, "Why can't you make good grades like your brother?" Then you feel as if you are the only one in the world who can't do things right. You may even feel that your parents love your brothers and sisters more than they love you. Even when your parents do not say such things, you will probably still find yourself feeling jealous of your brothers and sisters at times.

It may surprise you to know that sibling rivalry usually lasts into adulthood. It can be a good thing, because it teaches you a healthy amount of competition.

Too much competition, however, can be harmful. You will probably always feel some jealousy toward your brothers and sisters. You don't have to be guilty about having such feelings. You probably have good feelings toward your brothers and sisters more often than bad ones.

Having both good and bad feelings toward a person is called *mixed feelings*. The hardest combination is when you both like and dislike a person at the *same* time. As you grow older, you will learn to live with mixed feelings and you will select your companions for those qualities you like and be able to ignore the shortcomings that you don't like. Can you imagine how dull the world would be if everyone were perfect?

It sometimes happens in families that there is serious trouble. Your family's problems are not something you can easily avoid. If one of your brothers or sisters is in trouble, you will feel the tension at home. If someone in the house is ill, you will have to be considerate of that person. You may sometimes feel guilty that you don't feel very considerate. You may even resent the fact that the person in trouble seems to get more sympathy than you do. Everyone has these feelings. They are natural.

If this kind of feeling is making you tense, try getting

109

out of the house for awhile. Your neighborhood probably has an after-school center or a "Y" where you can work off some energy by swimming or playing basketball. Your neighborhood public library is a good place to read or study or listen to records quietly. If there is trouble in the family that you cannot handle by yourself, try talking it over with an understanding adult or a friend. You may find that teachers are more sympathetic to your problems than you think.

If your problems don't go away, see your school counselor, who is trained to help, and who will respect your privacy. For instance, if you find out that one of your brothers or sisters is using drugs, you should immediately seek help from the counselor.

Drug abuse is a complicated issue. Your brother, for example, may tell you that you can help him by getting him some money. What if he used your money to buy some poisoned narcotic drug and died? The counselor at school will be able to give you advice and information about such programs as Daytop Village, Phoenix House, Odyssey House, Synanon, or other groups that help addicts.

Study Aids

I. Understanding Your Brothers and Sisters

Some of the statements that follow are incorrect. Rewrite the sentences that are false to make them true. Do not simply insert words such as "not," "don't," "isn't," etc.

   a. Parents should not compare you to your brothers and sisters.
   b. If we truly like someone, we will never have any hard feelings toward them.
   c. An easy way to avoid family problems is to ignore them.
   d. Competition between brothers and sisters is normal.
   e. If a friend of yours is on drugs, and asks you for money, you might as well give it to him.
   f. Sibling rivalry is the name for competitive behavior between brothers and sisters.

II. Talking It Over

1. Melissa had to share her room with her 9-year-old sister, who was always snooping through Melissa's dresser drawers. Her mother wouldn't do anything about it. She told Melissa that her sister wouldn't take anything—she was only curious. If you were Melissa, how would you handle the situation?

2. Robert and Al were talking about their families. Robert had three brothers and two sisters, and Al was an only child. Robert said he wished he could be like Al, and have a room of his own with no one to bother him. Al said being an only child wasn't all that good. He wished he had an older brother to show him things, or even a younger brother to fight with once in a while. Do you agree with Robert or Al? Explain why.

3. Andy's younger sister, Elaine, always did better in school than he did. His parents were always telling him he was a disgrace to the family. The teachers in school sometimes asked him if he was her brother, which bothered him because he felt they were surprised he was so dumb. Actually, his grades weren't that bad. It's just that his sister's grades were always better. But as a result, he stopped studying altogether and began to think of things he could do that would make his family feel sorry for him. What advice would you give him?

Chapter 3
Helping Your Family Understand You

*We were at the table. Mother, Robert,
Mitch, and me. Mitch sat down at Daddy's place.
So I said, "Mitch, that's Daddy's place."*

*"Not any more," he said with a big Mouth
Watering Grin.*

"Move," I said.

Just gave me another MWG.

"Move!"

*"Stop that, Trissy," Mother said. "Mitch
can sit anywhere he wants."*

*"But he doesn't belong in that place." I was
so mad I was practically jumping up and down.*

*"Don't raise your voice at me," Mother said.
"You respect me. I'm your mother!"*

*"I'm your daughter! Why don't you respect
me? Why don't you tell Mitch to get out of Daddy's
seat? Why do you always get mad at me? Why is
MITCH always right? Why am I always wrong?
What's the answer?"*

*"You're rude, young lady! You leave the
table and don't you come back till you are prepared
to talk and act like a civilized person."*

So I left. I pounded as I went up the stairs....

from *I, Trissy,* Norma Mazer (NY: Delacorte Press, 1971)

Greg Henderson and his sister Martha, who was two
years younger, were fighting. "You said I could ride your
bicycle," said Martha.

"I never said any such thing," said Greg.

A voice came from another room. "Greg Henderson,
when will you learn to pick your clothes up off the floor?

113

And you, Martha, why must you be such a slob?" It was their mother.

Their father came in with Billy, the baby. Billy was three years old. He ran up to Greg and Martha and pushed the bicycle over. It fell against a table and knocked over a lamp.

"I told you never to bring that bicycle into the apartment," said Mr. Henderson.

"It would be stolen if I left it on the street," said Greg.

"Yes," said his mother, "I told Greg he could bring it into the house if he was careful."

The result of this little situation was a tremendous fight. Everyone began screaming, including little Billy.

Family fights are very common in many people's homes. Can they be avoided? What causes them? Often, the causes of family fights are an upset or tired mother or father, and children who do not listen to each other.

By listen, we do not mean "obey." By listen, we

mean just that—listen. What is the other person really saying? What does the other person really mean?

Dealing with others is a skill that should be learned in the home but often is not. It takes skill to understand what other people are all about, and to say the right thing clearly. The family is a good place to start practicing that skill because you live with your family and see them all the time. If you know anyone well, it should be the people with whom you live. If you understand them and they understand you, your life will be happier.

What could the Henderson family have done to avoid the free-for-all fight that was about to develop when we left them? Mrs. Henderson was obviously annoyed with her son Greg. And with good cause. He had left his clothes all over the floor for her to pick up. He could have gone in and picked them up himself. He could have just forgotten the fight with his sister. He knew she was only trying to get his attention anyway.

He could have told his mother that he would try to

keep his things neat. He should have known from the past that this would satisfy her.

Mrs. Henderson's annoyance with Martha was probably just a carry-over from her annoyance with Greg. If Martha had thought about this, she would not have let herself get upset. Shouting back at someone who is already angry never solves anything. Martha should have realized this.

If Greg and Martha had stopped their argument, they would have been able to prevent little Billy from imitating them by pushing the bicycle over.

What about the rules for the bicycle that Mr. and Mrs. Henderson disagree on? The family council is a good place to discuss such rules. Everyone should have an opportunity to express the way he feels about family matters without fear. A family that makes time to discuss rules will be a lot more peaceful than a family in which rules are made up on the spot.

A great mistake that some teen-agers make is asking their parents to explain rules when the parents are angry. "You never said what time I had to come in," said Betty, walking in at two o'clock in the morning. When your parents are angry, it is not the time to ask them to justify their rules. Try to understand their anger even if you disagree with it. If you are at fault, explain to them that you will try to do better the next time. If they are at fault, try to understand the way they feel.

All of this sounds like a lot of work. It is. You have to keep trying the psychological approach before you can make it work for you. Don't give up on it too easily. If your home life is not as happy as you want, you may be able to help out. You are a part of your family. You are needed there.

Study Aids

Understanding Helping Your Family Understand You

Some of the statements that follow are incorrect. Rewrite the sentences that are false to make them true. Do not simply insert words such as "not," "don't," "isn't," etc.

a. Shouting back at someone who is already angry is a good way to win a fight.

b. The family council is a good place to discuss rules.

c. A mistake teen-agers make is to explain rules when their parents are happy.

d. Family fights are common in most homes.

e. Understanding other people and saying the right thing clearly comes naturally.

f. If you understand your family, and they understand you, your life will be happier.

II. *Talking It Over*

1. Paul was ten years old, and his brother Sid was eight. One day Paul was building a model airplane. Sid asked if he could help. Paul said no. Sid took some pieces of Paul's airplane and threw them on the floor. Paul hit his brother. Sid began to cry loudly. Paul's mother ran in, hit Paul for making Sid cry, and hit Sid for making a mess. Do you think she did the right thing? How would you handle the situation? Was Paul right to hit Sid? How could each person have improved his actions?

2. Sue got permission to use the family car. She picked up several friends, and drove 50 miles to the beach. Sue and her friends had a great time at the beach. They didn't leave until after five. The traffic was heavy, and Sue didn't get home until 7:30. Her parents had made plans to go to a 7 o'clock movie. They were furious and told Sue she couldn't use the car for a month. Sue couldn't understand their anger, because they had given her permission to use the car. Why were Sue's parents angry? Was Sue right or wrong? Were her parents right to be angry? How could they have prevented this problem?

Unit V

Drugs and What They Do To You

Chapter 1
Alcohol

*The crowd kept growing. It seemed like
everyone in town knew that today was the
championship game. People pushed and, I swear,
I must have had three elbows jammed into my side.
But one guy was worse than any other. This big
mouth in a trench coat was really plastered. Maybe
he wasn't a bad guy, but he sure was drunk. He was
noisy and smelled terrible. He made everyone
nervous but, more than anything, he kept picking
on this black kid.*

*He kept cursing at him but the black kid
just kept his place in line and tried to ignore him.
It was amazing the way he would just stand there.*

*The crowd had watched and listened to all
this for a long time. Then they got mad. I don't
know if it was the long wait, the drunk himself, or
the way he was picking on the kid. Whatever it was
—the people in the crowd—blacks and whites—went
after the drunk. . . .*

The alcohol that people drink usually comes from
grains or fruit that have been *distilled* or *fermented*. The
most common type of alcohol is made by mixing grains with
yeast to make a mash. *Fermentation* is the chemical reaction
that takes place in the mash, changing part of the grain to an
alcohol called *ethanol*.

"Hard" liquors are usually manufactured by
distilling the alcohol made by fermentation. The ethanol is
boiled and the vapor is carried through tubes and condensed.

Distillation takes out most of the water and increases the percentage of alcohol in the liquid. When this liquid is aged in wooden barrels, liquor such as bourbon or Scotch results.

For thousands of years, people all over the world have drunk wine. Most wines are made from grapes, although other fruits can be used. The grapes are gathered, placed in large vats, covered with sugar, and crushed. The juice mixes with sugar, causing a chemical reaction to begin. After about nine days, the natural bacteria in the sugared grape juice causes it to ferment. The juices are then strained off and put into casks or bottles and allowed to age.

Beers are made from grains (usually barley) flavored with *hops* mixed with yeast. Once this mixture has fermented, the fluid is drawn off and bottled or canned under pressure.

Beers and wines usually have an alcohol content of from 3% to 12%. "Hard" liquors may have from 30% to 60% alcohol in them.

How much alcohol can a person drink? How much will make them drunk? How much is harmful? These are questions that are natural for people your age to ask. Perhaps you have already experimented with drinking, with or without the knowledge of your parents. Perhaps you come from a home where it is customary for the older children to drink some wine with meals. Still, a young adolescent who has had a lot of experience drinking a great deal of alcohol is rare. Such a person may already be on the road to a drinking problem.

The amount of alcohol in the blood can be measured scientifically. A person with more than 0.15% alcohol in his blood is considered intoxicated. The figure will vary slightly for persons with different body structures. A person who has had two strong drinks may already have this much alcohol in his blood. The alcohol will be absorbed into the bloodstream more slowly if it is drunk with a meal or after a meal.

After alcohol is absorbed by the body, it is concentrated in the nerves and brain. Its effect is as a *depressant*, meaning that it slows down the mental processes. These include not only thinking, but the body's reaction time. It will take you longer to perform any task under the influence of alcohol and your chances of making a mistake are much greater. For this reason, driving after drinking any amount of alcohol becomes more dangerous. Every year, more than half of all deaths in automobile accidents are caused by drivers who have been drinking.

One of the most harmful effects of alcohol is that use of it by some people can cause *alcoholism*. Alcoholism is a disease that causes heavy and uncontrollable drinking.

A true alcoholic may once have been only a "social drinker." But by gradually increasing his use of alcohol, the alcoholic has become addicted to it. He stays *intoxicated*, or

123

drunk, because the alcohol level in his blood is always high enough to cause a state of drunkenness. His body never has time to get rid of the alcohol.

The real alcoholic cannot face the world unless his mind is blurred by alcohol. Because of some problem, real or imagined, he prefers not to face reality. The alcoholic is a sick person. His illness is as real as if it were cancer or heart disease. Alcoholism must be treated as both an emotional and physical disease.

Let's examine the case history of an alcoholic.

John was a happily married man with one small son and a pretty wife. He had always been a moderate social drinker. He did not drive his car when he had been drinking. He had an occasional drink after work, went to cocktail parties, and sometimes drank wine with his meals. He was in no sense a "problem" drinker. Then his company was sold to a large corporation and he lost his good job.

Because he was past forty years of age, John found it fairly difficult to find new work immediately. He began to drink a bit more heavily. He finally found a job, but it was not in a field that interested him. His work became very uninteresting to him. It was only a way of making enough money to feed his family.

John found that he looked forward to finishing work at five o'clock and having several drinks. His "several" drinks increased to several more. He began to sit and drink all evening, ignoring his family. The money he was making at his new job was not really enough to pay for both his family's needs and the drinks that were becoming increasingly important.

Then he began to arrive late to work. He missed a day of work, then another, and then another. He had severe hangovers and began to drink in the morning to cure them. Finally he lost his job. His boss, who had seen the problem, realized that alcohol was the cause. When he tried to talk to John about alcoholism, John muttered something angrily and walked away.

John still had his need for alcohol, but now he had no job and no money. His wife became disgusted with him. His small son could not understand why a father who had once loved him very much and spent a lot of time with him was now seldom at home. When John did come home, he ignored the little boy and acted very strangely. John's wife took her son and went to live with her parents. She got a job so that she could support herself. Now John was left totally alone.

Many alcoholics reach this point. Some become complete derelicts and find a "home" on "skid row." Others attempt suicide, end up in hospitals or jail, or are sent to mental institutions.

Many alcoholics die because of the physical damage caused by the overuse of alcohol. Alcoholism causes many ailments. A large number of alcoholics suffer from malnutrition because they spend so much time drinking that they fail to eat properly. Alcoholism also may cause severe mental illness, such as *delerium tremens* (d.t.'s), which are frightening hallucinations. Other illnesses that can result from alcoholism include *cirrhosis* of the liver and inflammation of the stomach, which leads to ulcers.

What can be done about alcoholism? What could be done for John? The answers are many, but there is no one complete answer. Many social problems have no answers.

If John had never taken a drink, there would have been no problem. If he had had help when he lost his job, he might have been able to face and solve his problems, rather than try to escape them by drinking. Prevention is always better than cure where alcoholism is concerned. However, when prevention fails, people do become alcoholics. What is the cure?

One answer is "Alcoholics Anonymous." In any city in the United States, an alcoholic or his friends or family may contact this organization. All of the AA's members have at one time or another been alcoholics or problem drinkers. When contacted, the organization will send a representative who is a former alcoholic to talk to the sick person or his family. The representative will try to decide whether the alcoholic's problem is serious enough to require medical help, social help, psychological help, or a combination of all three.

In any case, the alcoholic no longer feels totally alone. He is being helped by a large organization. With professional medical guidance, a program will be developed for him. If he needs to have someone with him to prevent him from drinking, members will talk to him and help him to resist the physical need for alcohol. If he stays with the program, the alcoholic eventually becomes well again. His mind clears. He is able to go back to work. The horror of alcoholism is in the past. He is able once more to join society, though he cannot drink again, even moderately. Often he, too, as a member of Alcoholics Anonymous, will be able to help other people with drinking problems.

Study Aids

I. *The Vocabulary of Psychology*

Each word in the left column has a definition in the right column. In your notebook write the number of the word on the left and match it with the letter of its definition.

1. fermentation   a. slow down the mental processes
2. depressant   b. the chemical reaction that takes place in whiskey mash
3. alcoholism   c. a disease which causes those who have it to drink heavily
4. intoxicated   d. process by which "harder" liquors are made
5. distilling   e. drunk

II. *Understanding Alcoholism*

Some of the statements that follow are incorrect. Rewrite the sentences that are false to make them true. Do not simply insert words such as "not," "don't," "isn't," etc.

a. Beer is made from grapes.
b. Alcohol will be absorbed into the bloodstream more slowly if it is drunk with a meal.
c. Alcohol speeds up the body's reactions.
d. Many alcoholics end up in hospitals or jail.
e. All members of Alcoholics Anonymous have at one time or another been alcoholics.

III. *Talking It Over*

1. Ann's mother was an alcoholic. When Ann came home from school, her mother was usually sleeping. Her

127

mother hardly ever did the housework, or cooked, or washed and ironed the laundry. Ann hated her mother. She never invited friends home after school. She was very ashamed of her mother. Were Ann's feelings wrong? Explain your answer. What could Ann have done about her situation? Was her mother acting this way on purpose? What advice would you give to Ann?

2. Bob was in the ninth grade. He and his friends started to experiment with alcohol. They bought some cheap wine and got drunk. Bob felt great. Pretty soon, he wanted to drink wine all the time. He began to buy pints of wine in the morning and get drunk instead of going to school. Bob's friends no longer wanted to hang out with him. Why? Was Bob an alcoholic? Discuss your answer with the class.

3. Don and Rusty saw a man in the park who was drunk. He was stumbling around, and mumbling to himself. Then he tripped and fell. The man couldn't get up by himself. Don and Rusty laughed at the man. They walked away from him. Did they do the right thing? Why? What would you have done?

Chapter 2
Tobacco

Dear Alan,

I never thought I'd have to say this to my older brother, but you were right. Smoking is a really dumb thing to do. Joey and I found that out yesterday.

We decided that we'd look really cool if we smoked. But we figured that before we smoked in public we could use some practice first. So we went over to Joey's house after school. No one was home, so we took three of Mr. Foster's cigarettes. Then we went up to Joey's room. It took us about fifteen minutes to get the first one lit, and we practically burned off our fingers first. Then Joey dropped the cigarette on the bed, and it rolled onto the floor. By the time we found it, it had made a burn in the rug. Boy, did that smell! After that, we took turns puffing on the cigarette. It took all my willpower to keep from coughing. The thing sure tasted awful. I kept thinking I'd get used to it, and I kept saying, "Boy, this is really great." And Joey kept saying, "Yeah, it sure is." But he didn't look like he meant it.

When we finished the first cigarette, we lit the second one right away. Instead of getting better, the taste was getting worse. I was so dizzy I had to lean against the wall to keep from falling down. Joey didn't look so hot. He looked sort of like he was going to throw up. Finally, Joey said, "You don't look very cool." I said, "Neither do you." Then we both started to laugh. We didn't even light the third cigarette.

I think I'll tell Mom and Dad that I decided never to smoke. But I don't think I'll tell them why.
Your brother,
Bob

You may have read the story of Sir Walter Raleigh's coming to North America in the early colonial period, and finding that the Indians burned a "noxious weed" and "sucked its smoke." The noxious weed he wrote about was tobacco. The early explorers were fascinated by the way the Indians used this weed. They burned and smoked this plant in strange pipes that they hooked through their noses or put into their mouths.

Soon the explorers tried smoking, themselves. They found it pleasant. After they sat with a pipe for a while, they seemed to feel more relaxed.

The settlers got some of the tobacco from the Indians and sent it back to England. Soon tobacco became well known in Europe. Tobacco houses or "pipe houses" became popular places where men went to buy tobacco and sit and smoke their pipes. The use of that "noxious weed" spread swiftly over the entire world.

Today, most of the tobacco grown is used in cigarettes. The Surgeon General of the United States has established connections between cigarette smoking and several serious diseases, including lung cancer. Strangely enough, statistics show that moderate smoking of cigars does not seem to affect health as much as the same amount of cigarette smoking. Pipe smoking is also less dangerous than cigarette smoking, although pipe smokers have a higher than average number of cases of mouth and throat cancer.

No matter how tobacco is used, it acts as a mild *narcotic*. A narcotic is a drug that relieves pain and makes you sleepy. It slows down bodily functions, including the heartbeat, the circulation of the blood, and the processes of the brain. All this is caused by a poison in the tobacco called *nicotine*. Taken by itself, even in small amounts, nicotine can have severely harmful effects.

The nicotine and tar in tobacco may accumulate in the body until a *carcinogenic* reaction is caused. A carcinogenic reaction is a chemical change in a normal body cell that changes it into a cancer cell. The cancer cell multiplies quickly and spreads throughout the body.

There is no doubt that nicotine and tobacco tars contribute to changes in heart action. The occurrence of heart disease in smokers is almost five times greater than in non-smokers. The tobacco and nicotine also seem to cause changes in the glands that control the action of the heart, causing heart stoppages and other heart ailments.

Less dangerous skin cancers are sometimes caused by the heat from a pipe, cigar, or cigarette in the mouth. The cancer may start as a small, hard pimple on the lips or tongue. Skin cancer generally has a lower death rate than lung cancer, but it is still a serious disease.

Since 1960, much controversy has been raised about how far a country may go to protect its citizens from dangers to their health. For 300 years, tobacco has been a major source of income in the United States, particularly in the South. Legislators were reluctant to take action against the use of tobacco because so many people's livelihoods depend upon the industry and scientists until now had not agreed upon the effects. Thus we had the unusual situation of one government agency—the Surgeon General—condemning the use of tobacco, while another—the Department of Agriculture—was encouraging the growing of tobacco by paying money to tobacco farmers.

However, with the huge increase in death rates from lung cancer and other tobacco-related diseases, and with modern research demonstrating more and more convincingly the connection between smoking and lung cancer, some legislation was finally passed. All cigarette packages must now carry a warning that cigarettes are dangerous to health. Further legislation limits the advertising of cigarettes and requires that tobacco companies continue to point out the danger associated with tobacco.

The warning about tobacco is clear. If you are not smoking, you should not begin. If you are smoking, you should quit. The harmful effects of tobacco can be reversed in people who have quit smoking. Any other direction leads to a probable shortening of your life.

100,000 DOCTORS HAVE QUIT SMOKING CIGARETTES

Study Aids

I. The Vocabulary of Psychology

1. Each word in the left column has a definition in the right column. In your notebook write the number of the word on the left and match it with the letter of its definition.

1. tobacco	a. a chemical reaction that changes a normal cell into a cancer cell
2. carcinogenic	b. a drug that relieves pain and makes you sleepy
3. nicotine	c. a poison in tobacco
4. narcotic	d. a noxious weed

2. Write the letters *a* through *d* in your notebook. Next to each letter, write the word or words from question 1 that correctly belong in the blank spaces in each of the following statements.

a. A _____ slows down bodily functions, including the heartbeat, the circulation of the blood, and the processes of the brain.

b. _____ was gotten from the Indians and sent back to England.

c. Taken by itself, _____ can have severely harmful effects.

d. Nicotine and tar may accumulate in the body until a _____ reaction is caused.

II. Understanding Tobacco

Some of the statements that follow are incorrect. Rewrite the sentences that are false to make them true. Do not simply insert words such as "not," "don't," "isn't," etc.

a. Pipe smoking is more dangerous than cigarette smoking.

b. Tobacco is a mild narcotic.

c. Legislators were slow to take action against the use of tobacco because they all used it.

d. Skin cancer has a higher death rate than lung cancer.

e. The Department of Agriculture encouraged the growing of tobacco by paying money to tobacco farmers.

III. *Talking It Over*

1. Mr. and Mrs. Adams went to visit Mr. and Mrs. Johnson. Mr. Adams lit a cigarette and looked around for an ashtray. When he couldn't find one, he asked Mrs. Johnson where they were kept. She replied that she didn't have any ashtrays in the house because she didn't approve of smoking. Mr. Adams was embarrassed and angry. Why? Was Mrs. Johnson right in feeling the way she did? How could the situation be handled more tactfully?

2. Many teen-agers don't take up the habit of smoking, although their parents and older brothers and sisters may smoke. Why? Should these teen-agers try to convince members of their family not to smoke? How can they do this without stepping on people's feelings?

3. Dave started to smoke cigarettes when he was eleven. By the time he was thirteen, he was taking drugs and drinking, also. Is there a relationship between smoking, drinking, and taking drugs? Discuss.

Chapter 3
Psychedelics, Narcotics, Stimulants, and Others

I got tired of the gang. You see, a while before they threw me out of the block, out of the club, all the little kids were smoking pot. Little guys, eight and nine years old. Well, that got me, and then, one day, I saw that there were boys sitting out there by the baker passing things back and forth. Little kids would come and pay them money and they would get pot. I didn't want that. I never took pot. I didn't want my little brother to do it or those little kids there, either.

Like when I go to my school there are a lot of boys who do it, a lot of boys from my neighborhood who are in the school. I figure out that maybe those boys in my school who lived on my block were buying from the boys in the school and selling it some. Of course, I couldn't prove anything, but all I knew was tnat all of a sudden the little kids on the block were having it. So I figured out for myself that there's a time to tell and a time to keep quiet, and I figured that my time to tell had come. Or else I'd see my own little brother walking around with pot. So I told the policeman, but I told him not to tell my name. They got those boys and some of them they sent away and some of them they didn't...

from *Two Blocks Apart*, Charlotte Mayerson, ed. (NY: Holt, Rinehart & Winston, Inc., 1965)

When people speak of the "drug problem," they generally are not talking about alcohol and tobacco. Yet both of these are, in fact, drugs, and the same arguments against smoking and drinking apply to the misuse of other drugs.

The arguments are: 1) they can be habit-forming, or *addictive*, and 2) they can damage and destroy your mind and body.

Yet people continue to smoke and drink.

And people continue to take other drugs.

Why? Because, in some cases, the habit-forming effects have already taken over. We are all familiar with the cigarette smoker who coughs all day long and reaches for another cigarette to stop the cough. Almost as familiar is the "pothead," who tells everybody that he smokes pot just for kicks, and could stay off it anytime he wanted. However, he smokes it to take a test, to watch television, to go to class, to go to sleep, and finally can hardly do anything without having to get "stoned" first. He gets "stoned," he thinks, "so he can enjoy it more," or "so he can do better on the test." But he is really just lying to himself.

The cases of the cigarette smoker and the pot smoker described above are both examples of *psychological addiction*. This means that the taking of the drug gets to be a habit that the user depends on. He needs it to face life.

The other kind of addiction is *physiological addiction*. This occurs with such drugs as heroin, morphine, and other drugs that are made from opium. In this type of addiction, the body cannot get along without a regular dose of the drug. If the drug user cannot get his "fix," or dose, he suffers *withdrawal symptoms*. These include severe headaches, vomiting, nausea, muscle spasms, the "shakes," and extreme nervousness.

However, both these types of addiction result only after continued use of the drug, over a period of time. A heroin user may become addicted with only a few shots. It usually takes quite a bit longer to become addicted to alcohol. What causes the user to begin taking the drug in the first place? Why do people smoke cigarettes? Shoot heroin? Why would anybody begin taking into their body a substance that would destroy it?

There are many reasons, of course. Some are hard to understand for someone who does not share the personality of the addict. Psychological research has shown that there may be certain types of people who have *addictive personalities*. These people are more likely than others to be alcoholics, drug addicts, or acquire some other addiction.

Basically, an addictive personality needs to be dependent. He hasn't developed the strength to deal with his own problems. He chooses drugs as an escape, because he cannot physically run away from the source of his problems. The source of his problems is himself.

Yet the addictive personality is not found in everyone who uses drugs regularly. Another explanation is needed.

The explanation is that people like to take drugs. Drugs make people feel good, at least for a while. People drink to relax. Then maybe they begin drinking more to forget their problems entirely, at least till the next morning.

Marijuana makes things seem very funny. Old movies on television that would ordinarily be boring, suddenly become a great source of entertainment to a person who is "stoned." It seems to the person under the influence of marijuana that food tastes better, that music is more enjoyable, and that the world is friendly.

LSD heightens sensations and brings on hallucinations. It causes thoughts and images to become weirdly distorted.

The heroin high comes with a sudden rush, like a dam bursting, and all at once the world has changed. The user is no longer sitting in a dirty bathroom, but in a palace. He has escaped. Until, that is, he comes down and begins looking for his next fix.

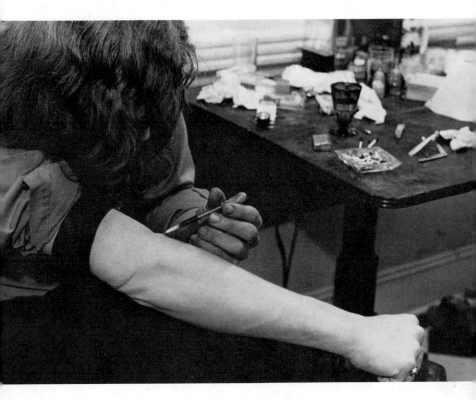

There are social reasons for taking drugs as well. The businessman enjoys having a few friendly drinks after work, as he and his friends talk over the affairs of the day. The 11-year-old glue sniffer enjoys the thrill of sitting in somebody's empty basement and passing the glue around to his friends as they "zonk" themselves senseless. It's hard to refuse a drug of any type when somebody offers it to you as a friendly gesture.

One problem alcoholics sometimes face is learning to refuse a friend who insists that "it's just one drink." Certainly, no one should insist that another person take a drink, a smoke, or a shot. And, on the other hand, no one should allow himself to be persuaded by a person who insists that he "try it just once."

The problem is to balance the good feeling that drugs give against the harmful effects. It's like a "buy now, pay later" plan. The temptation is to have the good feeling of drugs right now; maybe we won't have to pay later. This attitude is one of the things that makes drugs so appealing to young people. Young people are at their physical peak; they feel good. They can go for longer periods without proper food and rest than older people. They have a tendency to think that things will always be like this, and that nothing can be *that* harmful to them. Those kids you read about in the paper, dead from an overdose or sick from a bad batch of something—that's one case in ten thousand. So the thinking goes of someone who decides to experiment with drugs.

There is no answer to someone who thinks like that. There is no way to convince him that drugs will hurt him. It is impossible to convince the smoker who continues to smoke cigarettes that they are harmful. The evidence is already there. To someone who chooses to ignore the evidence, we can only say good luck.

Remember, there are many ways to feel good. Taking drugs may seem like one of them, but it may not be worth

the cost. People get "highs" from many activities—personal achievement, artistic and creative work, involvement in helping others. Don't let yourself be locked into the kind of thinking that makes drugs seem like the only way of life there is. There are many healthy ways to happiness.

The following chart summarizes some important facts about various drugs. It lists their effects, dangers, antidotes, symptoms, and medical uses.

NAME OF DRUG	REACTION ON BODY, BRAIN	HAZARDS, DANGERS
ETHYL ALCOHOL: *wine, beer, whiskeys,* etc.	relaxation, respiratory depression, distorted judgment, incoordination of movement, quarrelsomeness.	death from overdose, antisocial and homicidal behavior, irreversible damage to body tissues (brain, liver, pancreas, kidney, etc.).
HYPNOTICS: *Barbiturates* and Non-Barbiturates	similar to that of alcohol: depressant effect on central nervous system, psychologic dependence, slurred speech.	accidental death from over-dosage (alone or in combination with alcohol), irritability, moroseness leading to possible acts of violence.
TRANQUILIZERS: Miltown, Equanil, Librium, Valium	more selective than barbiturates in the relief of anxiety without impairing coordination of movement or affecting the judgment.	similar to those of barbiturates but reduced in intensity.
NARCOTICS: Opium, *codeine,* morphine, *heroin,* Demerol, Percodan	mental clouding, drowsiness, apathy, sometimes euphoria; reduced sex, hunger, and aggressive drives. With increased dosage tolerance develops so that addicts are able to take many times the normal lethal dose without significant effects—pleasurable or adverse. At this stage, the drugs are taken solely to prevent the withdrawal symptoms.	during early use there is a danger of accidental death from overdosage. Psychologic and physical dependence, reduced motivation, social deterioration, infection from the use of non-sterile injections, criminal activities to pay high cost of more and more narcotics.
TOBACCO: nicotine, carbon monoxide	low doses stimulate and high doses depress autonomic nervous system (the system which stimulates glands and smooth muscle), leading to constriction of blood vessels, increased blood pressure and heart rate.	with chronic use, cancer of the lungs, larynx, and mouth; bronchitis and pulmonary emphysema; damage to the heart, blood vessels and vision.
STIMULANTS (*"speed"*): *Amphetamines:* Methedrine, Dexedrine, Benzedrine, *cocaine,* Ritalin, caffeine	increased wakefulness, talkativeness, activity. Larger dose may produce irritability, aggressiveness, anxiety, paranoia, increased sweating and blood pressure, tremors of the hands.	sexually orgiastic experiences when taken intravenously. Overdosage rapidly achieved, with impairment of judgment, paranoia, possibly suicide.

142

ANTIDOTE	SYMPTOMS OF USE	MEDICAL USE
Empty stomach contents, administer hot black coffee, maintain body heat.	Nausea, vomiting, incoordination, slurring of speech, loss of inhibitions, aggressiveness.	To promote sleep and as a food source for energy (in limited cases).
Empty stomach contents, artificial respiration and other symptomatic support including maintenance of body heat.	Possible social deterioration, impulsiveness, violence. Smaller eye pupils after barbiturates, larger pupils after Doriden.	Used primarily to induce sleep and to reduce anxiety (tranquilize), to control chemically-induced convulsions, and occasionally as an aid in the diagnosis of psychiatric disorders.
As with hypnotics.	As with the hypnotics, although the minor tranquilizers seem less likely to be abused.	Anti-anxiety, sedative, muscle relaxant, anti-convulsant.
A narcotic antagonist such as nalorphine (Nalline) rapidly reverses the depressant effects but may unmask withdrawal symptoms in physically addicted persons.	Possible nausea and vomiting, hyperactivity, restlessness, anxiety, unresponsiveness to pain, lethargy.	Mainly to relieve pain, cough, diarrhea and as a preanesthetic medication (in part, to reduce anxiety, depression, and promote sleep).
Empty stomach contents; artificial respiration, and other symptomatic support as needed.	Discolored fingertips; cigarette cough.	None
Thorazine or Mellaril.	Dilated pupils, loss of appetite, over-activity, rapid speech, belligerence, suspiciousness, odd behavior.	To reduce appetite, overcome fatigue and sleepiness, improve mood, increase attentiveness and motivation for work and learning.

143

NAME OF DRUG	REACTION ON BODY, BRAIN	HAZARDS, DANGERS
MARIJUANA: Hashish, THC	absence of definite physiologic symptoms except perhaps reddening of eyes, and an increased heart rate.	high doses could cause anxiety, psychosis, neglect of personal hygiene, and social deterioration.
GLUE: solvents, deleriants, Toluene, xylene, benzene, gasoline, paint thinner, lighter fluid, etc.	Symptoms of drunkenness, dizziness, floating sensation. Intense feelings of well-being, feelings of increased power and aggressiveness. Visual hallucinations can occur, usually around themes of fire and heat. Recovery from small doses in 15 minutes to a few hours. Little physical dependence, although withdrawal symptoms (nausea, depression, loss of appetite) have been seen in heavy users. Moderate psychological dependence. Tolerance can develop after 3 months of continued weekly usage.	High concentration of toluene in the system may lead to permanent damage to the brain, bone marrow and, possibly, the liver and kidneys. Deaths from the inhalation of aerosol sprays have been reported. The aggressiveness produced by the use of glues can lead individuals into threatening situations.
PSYCHEDELICS: LSD-25, Mescaline, psilocybin, DMT, STP, DET, Hallucinogens, numerous others	Effect is on the central nervous system and the filtering mechanisms of the mind. They alter perception, intensify emotional reactions, and shift thinking to a dreamlike state. Individuals who are fearful and tense may have a severe panic reaction, and develop psychosis. Other individuals may resolve the conflicting feelings brought on by the drug. The experience is highly dependent on the conditions under which it takes place. Slight potential for psychological dependence; no physical dependence. Tolerance builds rapidly.	Potential hazards are psychological in nature, involving mood changes, panic, depressive and paranoid reactions, impairment of normal motivation, and sometimes prolonged psychotic reactions. Flashbacks (recurrences of effects without further use of drugs) have been reported, particularly when the individual is placed in a stress situation similar to the original drug experience.

144

ANTIDOTE	SYMPTOMS OF USE	MEDICAL USE
Limit stimulations from environment (darken lights, turn down music, close the eyes). Comforting the subject is also helpful.	Euphoria without drastic impairment of judgment or gait; reddening of eyes, dreamy state.	None
Artificial respiration.	Strong odor of glue or the other chemicals, symptoms of drunkenness: slurred speech, uncoordinated physical actions.	None; too toxic for use.
Same as with marijuana. "Talking-down" when done by a highly experienced person is preferred. Use of tranquilizers may be psychologically harmful and increase the chance of flashbacks.	Dilated pupils, hilarity, emotional highs and lows, nausea and vomiting (with peyote), increased pulse and blood pressure (primarily with DMT).	No validated uses have been proven. Possible application may be for the resolution of highly emotional conflict situations.

Study Aids

I. *The Vocabulary of Psychology*

1. Each word or phrase in the left column has a definition or an explanation in the right column. In your notebook write the number of the word or phrase on the left and match it with the letter of its definition or explanation.

1. psychological addiction
2. addictive
3. physiological addiction
4. withdrawal symptoms
5. addictive personality

a. habit-forming
b. severe headaches, vomiting, nausea, the shakes, and extreme nervousness
c. the taking of the drug is a habit the user depends on to help him face life
d. people who are more likely to become alcoholics or drug addicts
e. the body cannot get along without a regular dose of a drug

2. Write the letters *a* through *e* in your notebook. Next to each letter, write the word or words from question 1 that correctly belong in the blank spaces in each of the following statements.

a. Morphine and heroin users will develop a _____ _____ after continued use of these drugs.
b. Alcohol, tobacco, and heroin can all be _____ .
c. If the drug user cannot get his fix, he will suffer _____ .
d. Cigarette smoking and pot smoking are habits that can lead to _____ .
e. An _____ needs to be dependent.

II. Understanding Psychedelics, Narcotics, Stimulants, and Others

Some of the statements that follow are incorrect. Rewrite the sentences that are false to make them true. Do not simply insert words such as "not," "don't," "isn't," etc.

 a. The arguments against smoking, drinking, and taking drugs are 1) they are addictive and 2) they are illegal.

 b. Psychological addiction occurs with such drugs as heroin and morphine.

 c. A person with an addictive personality hasn't developed the strength to deal with his own problems.

 d. It seems to a person who is under the influence of heroin that food tastes better.

 e. There are social reasons for taking drugs.

 f. People can get high from activities other than drinking and taking drugs.

III. Talking It Over

1. Kenny had once been a straight 'A' student. He was energetic and fun to be with. He and his brother George were very close. Then, George began to notice that Kenny always seemed tired and irritable. His grades dropped to 'D's and 'F's. George wanted to help his brother. What do you think was wrong with Kenny? How could George help him?

2. Alice began taking pills and LSD when she was fourteen. By the time she was sixteen, she had had enough bad experiences to realize that drugs were not for her. She stopped taking drugs completely. But her friends were still taking drugs. They made fun of her. Then they got angry at her. Alice didn't know what to do. Because of her past, she thought that "straight" kids wouldn't want to be friends with her. Do you think she was right? Why were her old friends now acting so strangely to her? Discuss several things Alice could do.

Unit VI

You Become an Adult

Chapter 1
Entering Maturity

My older sister Ellie once said that I'm not interested in boys and that it's not normal. I acted dumb and made believe I didn't have any idea what she was talking about. I mean, I didn't want to go into details. Because the truth of the matter is, I am interested in the opposite sex, very much interested. As a matter of fact, I'm ashamed to say how interested I really am. I could name lots of boys— men even—that I was interested in, although nothing ever came of it.

from "Twice I Said I Love You," by Teresa Giardina, first published in *Datebook Magazine*, Young World Press

Growth comes not in a steady, gradual way, but in shorter periods of intense activity. The period from birth to the age of about six years is one of great change, bodily growth, and learning. From the age of six until you reach adolescence, growth continues, but the changes are not as obvious.

Then, suddenly, comes adolescence, the next period of important changes. During adolescence, you become sexually mature. In the process of becoming mature, you first develop secondary sex characteristics.

In men, the secondary sex characteristics are hair on the face and body, a deep voice, and broad shoulders. In women, they are breasts, hair on the body, widening of the hips, and a rounded figure.

The primary sex organs become mature at this time. This means that the testes in males and the ovaries in females become active. Boys are now able to become fathers, and girls able to become mothers.

When girls become sexually mature, increased amounts of the sex hormones enter the bloodstream. Girls begin to menstruate. *Menstruation* occurs at the end of the monthly *hormonal cycle*. These hormones are chemicals produced by the endocrine glands. They regulate the activities of the body. Both men and women produce hormones, although they are of different types in male and female bodies.

In women, the hormonal cycle begins with the build-up of hormones. These hormones cause an *ovulation*. Ovulation is the release of a mature egg cell from the ovary glands. This takes place about two weeks after the cycle begins. If sexual intercourse takes place during this time, it is possible for a child to be conceived. Hormones also produce changes in the womb of the female, preparing it to receive the developing fetus, or unborn baby, after conception.

If conception does not take place, materials from the uterus are discharged during menstruation. Menstruation usually takes place once a month and lasts from three to six days. Young girls often are not regular in their menstrual periods at first.

Although the material coming from the uterus looks like blood, it is really mucus colored with blood.

During the period, a sanitary pad or a tampon is worn to absorb the material. Young girls who are able to use tampons find that they are able to carry on more of their normal activities, such as going to the beach, during their menstrual periods. It is important for a girl to get enough exercise during her periods so that healthy circulation is maintained. This helps to prevent cramps.

When boys become sexually mature, they often have "wet dreams" or *nocturnal emissions*. This is an involuntary discharge of *semen*, or sperm cell fluid, usually during sleep.

The testes, or male sex glands, have begun to produce semen, and when enough of the fluid builds up, it will be discharged in this way. This is a natural and normal process.

150

Sexual excitement in which the penis fills with blood and becomes erect and hard also happens more frequently during adolescence. Boys are more likely to have these *erections* at this time of life because they are more easily stimulated by the things they see and feel. They are sometimes embarrassed by an erection because they think it is easily noticeable through their clothes, but ordinarily it is not that obvious. This, too, is a normal happening in the period of growing up.

During adolescence, emotions are often very strong. Boys and girls begin to develop sexual feelings about the opposite sex. For some people, these feelings come later than for others. When they do come, however, these feelings should not be regarded as shameful. Sexuality is something that cannot be *repressed*, or denied, without the possibility of bad results. No human being is *asexual*. Asexual means without sex.

But sexuality, though you feel it very strongly at this time, is only part of the human story. One human need is certainly to love and be loved. But there are other human needs—the needs for achievement, accomplishment, and self-esteem. They are equally important.

Studies have been done on man and other animals. It was discovered that animals possess curiosity in proportion to intelligence. The sea sponge, a kind of animal, has almost no intelligence. It behaves in a set way. It takes in food, digests it, gets rid of waste matter, and reproduces. It does not do anything else.

151

The chimpanzee, an animal with a high intelligence, will explore the world around it, just out of curiosity. Human beings have even more of this inborn curiosity.

Now is the time in your life when you have the most energy and curiosity about the world. You should not think, just because your sexual feelings are so strong, that sex is all there is to the world. You should not let your sexual drives interfere with your exploration and discovery of the world around you.

Some people think that once they have gone through the physical maturing process they have become adults. There is more to it than that.

What does it take to be a man or woman, instead of

a boy or girl? One of the most important qualities is self-esteem. Self-esteem comes from within. When you can feel proud of your own qualities and characteristics, and not have to put others "down" in order to feel "up," then you have self-esteem. When you hear groups of teen-agers calling each other by nicknames like "fatty," "liver-lips," and other slurs, you know they feel insecure about themselves.

People must choose to act grown-up. No one can make them do it. To *feel* grown-up, happy, and satisfied is a personal decision. No one has happiness and contentment all the time. There are always more things to work for. But when you can say to yourself that you are content with the kind of person you are, that is a sign you are growing up.

Study Aids

The Vocabulary of Psychology

Each word or phrase in the left column has a definition in the right column. In your notebook write the number of the word or phrase at the left and match it with the letter of its definition.

1. nocturnal emission

   a. without sex

   b. sperm cell fluid

2. hormonal cycle

   c. unborn baby

   d. a discharge of mucus colored with blood that usually takes place once a month in women

3. ovulation

4. fetus

   e. denied

   f. involuntary discharge of semen, usually during sleep

5. erection

   g. begins with the buildup of hormones, that cause an ovulation

6. repressed

   h. sexual excitement in which the penis fills with blood and becomes hard

7. asexual

8. menstruation

9. semen

   i. the release of a mature egg from the ovary glands

II. *Understanding Maturity*

Some of the statements that follow are incorrect. Rewrite the sentences that are false to make them true. Do not simply insert words such as "not," "don't," "isn't," etc.

154

a. Growth comes in a steady, gradual way.
b. During adolescence, you become sexually mature.
c. Menstruation occurs at the end of the monthly hormonal cycle.
d. Only women produce hormones.
e. Ovulation is the release of the sperm cell fluid.
f. Wet dreams are an involuntary discharge of semen.
g. Animals possess curiosity in proportion to their size.

III. Talking It Over

1. When Betty got her first menstrual period, she became curious about the changes that were taking place in her body. She wanted to learn more about sex. Her parents seemed to avoid her questions. Her friends didn't know the answers. Why was Betty suddenly curious about these things? Was this normal? Why? How and where could Betty find the answers to her questions?

2. Sometime after his fourteenth birthday, Ralph found himself thinking about sex a lot of the time. He would get erections when he saw pretty girls, or daydreamed. Sometimes this would even happen in class. At night, he had wet dreams. He felt guilty and ashamed about this. He tried to make his sexual feelings go away. Why do you think Ralph felt that way? What would be some better ways for Ralph to deal with his sexual feelings?

Chapter 2
The Uses of Sexuality

I don't know when it was that we knew
we'd get married to each other, some time. We just
started talking about it, one day, as if we always
had. We were sensible, we knew it couldn't happen
right off. We thought maybe when we were
eighteen. That was two years but we knew we had
to be educated. You don't get as good a job, if you
aren't.

We weren't mushy either, like some people.
We got to kissing each other good-by, sometimes,
because that's what you do when you're in love. It
was cool, the way she kissed you, it was like leaves.
But lots of the time we wouldn't even talk about
getting married, we'd just play checkers or go over
old homework, or once in a while go to the movies
with the gang.

It was really a wonderful winter. I played
in every basketball game and she'd sit in the stands
and watch and I'd know she was there. You could
see her little green hat or her yellow hair. . . .

FROM: TOO EARLY SPRING by Stephen Vincent Benet Published by Holt, Rinehart and Winston Copyright, 1933, by The Butterick Company Copyright renewed © 1961, by Rosemary Carr Benet Reprinted by permission of Brandt & Brandt

You have learned that you are a sexual being. Trying to deny or repress this fact will harm you. What use, then, is your sexuality to you? Traditionally, sexuality simply has meant the production of children to make a new generation. Today, the world is over-populated, and scientists are arriving at new ideas in connection with sexuality.

Sexuality means an understanding of your role as a man or woman. In our modern society, women can play a role equal to men. This means that many women want to postpone having children, or choose not to raise a family so they can continue their education or careers. Most boys also want to complete their education before they become fathers and have to assume the responsibility for a family.

Most people in our society get married eventually. Statistics show that divorce rates are much higher for those couples who marry between the ages of 15 and 23 than for those who wait until they are older. One reason for the higher divorce rate of those who marry younger may be that young wives become bored or frustrated if they have not had more experiences before getting married and having children.

The question comes up about what to do with your sexual feelings before marriage. The traditional viewpoint has been that sexual feelings should not be acted upon before marriage. Many young couples today do, however, feel that they are responsible enough to handle sex before marriage.

There are a number of dangers to this viewpoint. Couples of fifteen and sixteen, although they may be in love and "going steady," also want to enjoy some of their new freedoms, explore the world, and continue their educations. An unwanted pregnancy can be a tragic event because either the boy or girl are not ready to take on the responsibilities of parenthood.

Being responsible enough to handle sex means, among other things, facing the risks ahead of time and deciding if they are worth taking. Ask yourself, "What do I really want from this relationship? Is it really worth it to me? Will it affect all the other things I want for myself?" Be selfish—be sure that what you do is something you, not the boy or girl you are going with, wants. If your feelings dictate, or already have dictated, complete sexual relations examine ways to minimize the chances you will be, or are taking. Whatever faith you belong to you may want to find out about those methods of avoiding pregnancy (*contraception*) open to you. Even if your religious beliefs do not rule out abortion, it is still the last, unhappy resort. Different states have different abortion laws. In states where it is illegal, abortion is not only psychologically disturbing, but dangerous, difficult to obtain, and expensive.

Get advice. Look around for the right person to advise you. And that person is not likely to be a member of your own group of friends who is probably in need of solving the same kinds of problems that you are. Most adults today are concerned, but they are not as shocked as their parents were at the idea of sexual relations before marriage. Your most useful source of information would be a doctor, nurse, social worker, psychologist, guidance counselor, clergyman, or other trained person whom you respect and feel you can trust to keep your confidence. And there is literature on the subject that you can read.

Pregnancy is not the only risk. There has been a great increase in venereal diseases in our country, recently.

158

The venereal diseases are mainly *syphilis* and *gonorrhea.* They are very serious diseases that are transmitted through sexual contact. Modern drugs are usually effective against these diseases if they are caught in time. However, some strains have become resistant to cure. It is important to see a doctor immediately if you develop a hard sore on your sex organs or have a painful discharge from your genitals.

The only sure way to keep from catching one of these diseases is not to have any contact with someone who is already infected. Of course, the person who has casual sexual relations with boys or girls is taking a greater chance than the person who is "going steady." But it is often difficult to tell who is infected, since the first symptoms will disappear by themselves in syphilis, even though the disease is still active and may cause death, paralysis, or mental illness years later.

All of these reasons are outside reasons. In other words, what about the feelings of the young couple? For example, Matthew and Janet were juniors in high school. They began dating. Soon they decided that they were in love and wanted to go steady. When Janet was asked why she loved Matthew, she said he was full of life and fun to be with. Matthew would talk about Janet's beautiful figure and long blond hair.

Aside from sex, Matthew and Janet had no common interests. He was interested in fixing cars and she liked sports. As a result, they spent most of their time together "making out." Soon they were "going all the way" regularly. Janet found that she was pregnant.

She was actually happy when she knew she was pregnant, because she thought that now Matthew would have to marry her. To her, marrying Matthew would be the greatest thing in the world.

But Matthew had other ideas. He suggested that Janet go to another state and have an abortion. Janet was horrified. Her religion forbade her to have an abortion, and

159

she thought she wanted the baby anyway.

Janet's mother found out she was having a baby. She became hysterical and called Janet names. Janet's father threatened to have Matthew put in jail if he didn't marry Janet. Matthew refused. He left town.

Janet had to go to a home for unwed mothers to have the baby. After it was born, she came back to her parents with it. Janet showed little interest in the baby, and her mother had to take care of it.

However, Matthew began to write her letters. Finally, he came back to town and married Janet when their child was one year old. But they are not a happy couple. They fight and argue all the time, and Matthew is out several nights a week. He is thinking about leaving Janet and their child again. Janet doesn't realize this, but continually complains because he never takes her anywhere. Most of her old friends are away at college or working.

Janet was never really in love with Matthew. She was in love with the idea of marriage. She thought getting married would make her an adult and solve all her problems. She thought, that because she and Matthew both enjoyed having sex, they would have a good marriage. She was wrong.

Teen-agers who date many different people are putting themselves in a good position to find the qualities that really appeal to them. Physical attraction is an important quality. It is not the only reason for choosing another person, however.

Having similar interests is very important. It is hard for some young couples to tell whether they do have similar interests because they have not explored enough to know what their real interests are.

A rewarding sexual life results from knowing your own body and its pleasure sensations. You should not be ashamed to explore and think about yourself and your sexual feelings in private. Most people masturbate. This is normal. It does not, as many old myths state, cause people to go crazy. It can be a release for pent-up sexual feelings when you are not yet prepared for a sexual relationship with another person.

Sexuality is expressed in more ways than by direct sexual contact. During adolescence, the interest in personal appearance shown by boys and girls is an expression of sexuality. Dancing and playing sports are both expressions of sexuality because they give you pleasure in your body. These pleasures are natural, and they should be enjoyed as often as possible. You are also expressing your personality and sexuality when you find out what kinds of clothes look good on you.

Study Aids

I. Understanding the Uses of Sexuality

Some of the statements that follow are incorrect. Rewrite the sentences that are false to make them true. Do not simply insert words such as "not," "don't," "isn't," etc.

a. Divorce rates are lower for those couples who marry between the ages of 15 and 23.

b. Venereal diseases are mainly syphilis and pneumonia.

c. The only sure way to keep from catching a venereal disease is not to have contact with someone who has one.

d. Dancing and playing sports are both expressions of sexuality.

e. Teen-agers who date many different people are fickle.

II. Talking It Over

1. Joe and Cindy had been dating for six months. For the last two months, they had been having sexual intercourse. One day, Joe noticed that it hurt when he urinated, and there was pus in his urine. Joe told this to his basketball coach. The coach called Joe a fool, and said Cindy was a tramp. What do you think was the matter with Joe? Do you agree with what the coach said? Why? Why did the coach say what he did? What should Joe do next?

2. Jesse and Lucy were going steady. They were having sexual intercourse. After a year, Lucy realized that she wasn't really in love with Jesse, and she broke off with him. Jesse was hurt. He told the guys at school that Lucy was an "easy mark." Was this true? Why? Soon, lots of guys were asking Lucy out and expecting her to have sex with them. What advice could you give to Lucy? Why did Jesse act as he did?

3. Paul's parents gave him a lecture on masturbation. They told him it was a terrible thing. They said people who masturbate go blind and crazy. Paul had been masturbating for the past six months. He began to get very worried. Were Paul's parents right in what they said? Why did they say it? What should Paul do now?

Chapter 3
The Development of Love

Seven Daffodils

I do not have a mansion,
I haven't any land,
Not even a paper dollar
To crinkle in my hand.

But I can show you morning
On a thousand hills,
And kiss you, and give you
Seven daffodils.

I do not have a fortune
To buy you pretty things,
But I can weave you moonbeams
For necklaces and rings.

And I can show you morning
On a thousand hills,
And kiss you, and give you
Seven daffodils.

—Seven golden daffodils,
All shining in the sun,
To light the way to evening
When our day is done.

And I will give you music
And a crust of bread,
A pillow of piney boughs
To rest your head.

I do not own a mansion,
I haven't any land,
Not even a paper dollar
To crinkle in my hand.

But I will show you morning
On a thousand hills,
And kiss you, and give you
Seven daffodils.

You have learned that your personality develops or goes through stages. It may surprise you to learn that the emotion called love is something that you learn and develop. The way you relate to other people is based on what you learned from your parents when you were a very small child.

There are three stages to early childhood. One is early infancy. In this stage, the child learns to love and trust his mother, who brings him food and changes his diaper. The first person the child relates to is his mother.

But a baby will also relate to his father if his father holds him and feeds him and bathes him. When men become fathers, they should help to take care of their children so

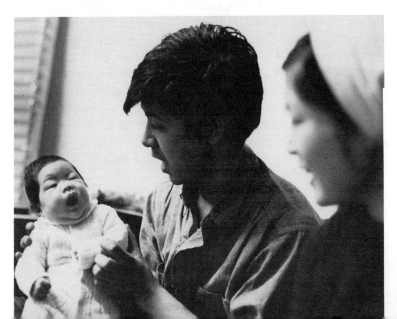

that their children will learn that love and gentleness are part of a man's personality.

The second stage of early childhood is the toddler stage. In this stage, the child learns to recognize strangers. Strangers usually make the baby fearful, and he cries and clings to his mother when they try to pick him up. At this stage, the mother teaches her baby to be less fearful of strangers. Mothers should allow their children to be held by friends and relatives to get the baby used to liking others.

The third stage of early childhood is the three-to-five-year old stage. The three to five year old learns by imitating the grownup people in his world. A boy will want to be like his father, a girl like her mother. Fairly often a boy of this age will insist he wants to marry Mommy, or a girl will want to marry Daddy. It is a natural pattern of growth. Understanding parents can help their children, at this stage, gain a sense of who they are, boy or girl, and what kind of adults they will be.

Children learn to love by passing through the stages of development with loving help from their parents. If a child's mother, for instance, has no husband, she should not speak badly of men. If she does, both her sons and daughters will have poor sexual guidance.

The way a child's parents behave toward each other influences the child's outlook. If parents are loving and respectful toward each other, the child will learn that a woman should be loving and respectful toward her husband and that a man should love and respect his wife.

In cases where a child's parents are not the ideal loving couple, or when there is no father or no mother in the home, the child can learn with guidance to understand that these are not the ideal conditions, and still grow up to experience the greatest of human emotions—love.

Study Aids

I. *Understanding the Development of Love*

Some of the statements that follow are incorrect. Rewrite the sentences that are false to make them true. Do not simply insert words such as "not," "don't," "isn't," etc.

a. The emotion called love is something everyone is born with.

b. There are five stages to early childhood.

c. The first person the child relates to is his brother.

d. Fathers shouldn't take care of their children for fear that they'll be called sissies.

e. It is natural for little boys to be in love with their mothers.

f. The ways a child's parents behave toward each other influences the child's outlook.

II. *Talking It Over*

1. Mrs. Turner's son Allen was two years old. She had never left him with a baby-sitter because she didn't trust anyone besides herself to take proper care of him. On their third anniversary, Mr. Turner insisted that they get a baby-sitter for Allen and go out to dinner. Mrs. Turner was very nervous all day. When it was time to leave, she hugged and kissed Allen as if she would never see him again. He screamed and cried as she went out the door. Mrs. Turner called the baby-sitter after a half hour, and when she learned Allen was still crying, insisted that they return home. Was she right to go home? Why? What could she have done to prepare Allen for a baby-sitter? What should Mrs. Turner have been teaching Allen at this stage of development? What kind of boy do you think Allen will be when he's older?

167

2. Dan was a very tall, muscular, athletic man. His son Ronnie was three. Dan had never helped his wife take care of Ronnie, because he thought that was woman's work. Dan did not want Ronnie to be a sissy. He wouldn't allow anyone to comfort Ronnie when he cried. He was very strict with Ronnie and spanked him a lot. When he spent time with Ronnie he tried to teach him games like baseball and football. What do you think of Dan's treatment of Ronnie?

3. Jerry's parents were divorced, and he lived with his mother. Jerry's parents had fought a lot before the divorce. Jerry's mother was always telling him what a terrible person his father was. Whenever Jerry visited his father, his mother said "don't come back" as he walked out the door. When he returned, she wanted to know everything his father had said and then criticized what his father had said. She constantly asked Jerry if he loved her better than his father. What could be the results of her behavior? How do you think her actions made Jerry feel? Discuss.

Chapter 4
Parenthood

I'll never forget the time I asked my dad what the most important thing in his life was. He said he remembered the death of his father and my birth more than anything else. I was touched to think I meant so much to him. And I know he loved his father very much.

Now that Gordon and I have a child I think I know what my father meant. I don't mean anything mystical about birth or death being related. But maybe they are.

But when Jeff was born I became somebody else or changed somehow. I wanted our son to have a good life. I knew it lay before him to mold it into whatever shape he wanted it to be. And I also know I was part of his life. I had to help him, to guide him. I was going to . . . I was going to.

When a man and a woman make love, they become sexually aroused. This means that certain changes take place in their bodies. These changes make it possible for the man to insert his penis into the woman's vagina. Sperm flows from his body into hers. This act is called sexual intercourse.

If intercourse takes place when the woman is in approximately the second week of her menstrual cycle, she is in a *fertile period* and can become pregnant. This means that an egg cell has been released by the ovaries and is ready to be fertilized by a sperm cell. One ejaculation or release of semen contains millions of sperm.

Each sperm cell has a tail which enables it to move. When one sperm cell reaches an egg, it penetrates the egg, and unites or joins with it. The tail drops off. The surface of the egg now becomes hard, and no other sperm cell can enter the egg. A full-grown baby will result from this beginning.

When the egg is fertilized, it comes to rest in the uterus or womb, which is attached to the vagina. In the uterus, the embryo (or developing baby) receives its nourishment from the mother through the *placenta*. Attached to the placenta is the *umbilical cord*. The umbilical cord, which is also attached to the baby's navel, connects the placenta and unborn baby.

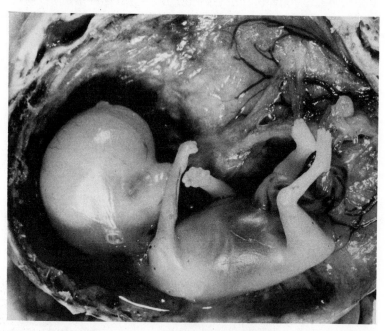

After about two months, the embryo begins to take the shape of a human being. Growth at this stage is so rapid that if the same rate of growth continued after the child was born, three-year-old children would weigh 50,000 pounds.

After about nine months, a fully developed baby is ready to be born. Muscle contractions begin within the mother's womb. They signal the beginning of birth, and are felt as labor pains by the mother. Gradually, the contractions increase in length and frequency. They push the baby into position to be born. Finally the baby is pushed out through the mother's vagina, or birth canal. The placenta and the umbilical cord follow soon after. They are called the *afterbirth*. The doctor cuts and clamps off the umbilical cord. Your "bellybutton" is the stump of the umbilical cord that once attached you to your mother's body.

Most babies are born in hospitals where their mothers can get help from doctors and nurses if they need it. Birth is a natural process, however, not a disease. Babies are healthier if their mothers take good care of themselves during pregnancy, getting the right foods and vitamins and enough rest. Diseases that may not be very serious to a grown person are very harmful to unborn babies. German measles is one such disease. It can cause birth defects. Pregnant women who have not had German measles should be careful to avoid anyone with this disease.

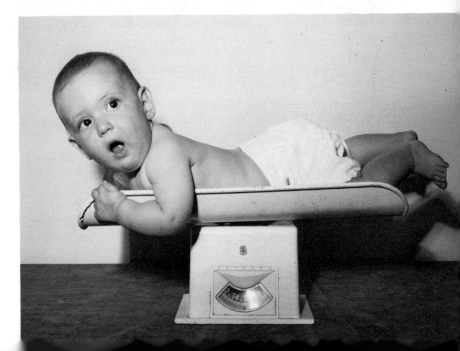

Newborn babies need a great deal of care and attention from their mothers and fathers, if they are to thrive. They are helpless and they need to be fed and cared for all the time. Newborn babies also need to be held and played with by their parents. If they do not get this contact, they will grow up with psychological difficulties that appear later in life. Young fathers are often of great help to their wives in taking care of new babies.

An activity that is gratifying and educational to teenagers is to spend time as volunteer workers, in nursery schools and day-care centers, children's hospitals, and orphanages, helping young children. Every experience with new-born babies is valuable, and very likely more enjoyable than most people would think.

You are not born to be a good parent. No one is. You must learn how—learn about feelings and emotions. Reading books like this one can tell you some things, but there is much that can be learned only from observing for yourself the ways people grow up. In this way you will be able to help your own children live better lives. Your own life will be more satisfying.

Study Aids

I. *The Vocabulary of Psychology*

Each word or phrase in the left column has a definition in the right column. In your notebook write the number of the word or phrase and match it with the letter of its definition.

1. ejaculation
   a. a time, approximately in the second week of her menstrual cycle, when a woman can become pregnant
2. umbilical cord
   b. release of semen
3. fertile period
   c. connects the placenta and the unborn baby
4. afterbirth
   d. the placenta and the umbilical cord that follow soon after the baby is pushed out
5. placenta
   e. the organ through which the embryo receives nourishment from the mother

II. *Understanding Parenthood*

Some of the statements that follow are incorrect. Rewrite the sentences that are false to make them true. Do not simply insert words such as "not," "don't," "isn't," etc.

a. If intercourse takes place when the woman is in a fertile period, she can become pregnant.
b. An ejaculation contains one sperm.
c. Each egg cell has a tail which enables it to move.

e. The umbilical cord is attached to the baby's navel.

f. The placenta and umbilical cord that follow after the baby is born are called the bellybutton.

g. German measles is very harmful to unborn babies.

III. *Talking It Over*

1. When Nellie discovered she was pregnant, she was too embarrassed to go to a doctor because she wasn't married. She didn't change her diet, but kept eating her favorite foods—pizza, potato chips, hot dogs, and soda. She usually stayed up until two or three in the morning, watching television. How will Nellie's behavior affect her baby? What suggestions about diet, sleep, and general health would you give Nellie?

2. If women who are heroin addicts continue to take the drug throughout their pregnancy, their babies will be born addicted to heroin also. Why do you think this is? How do you think this will affect the lives of these babies? Why?

3. Jim and Ellie were married right after graduating high school. Jim was working at a gas station. And Ellie, as a waitress, made a fair salary and extra money on tips. They saved, so that even when Ellie had to quit her job to have the baby, things were fine. But then when the baby was only a couple of months old, the gas station closed and Jim was out of a job. No money at all was coming in. Ellie's boss at the restaurant said that Ellie could come back to work for the dinner shift. It seemed like a good idea, at least until Jim could get located again. But could Jim take care of the baby? Would it be good for the baby? Would it be good for Jim? Discuss.

Pronunciation Guide

achievement	(uh-CHEEV-munt)
addictive	(uh-DIK-tiv)
adolescence	(AD-uh-LES-unz)
adrenal	(uh-DREE-nul)
affection	(uh-FEK-shun)
afterbirth	(AF-tur-burth)
alcoholism	(AL-kuh-hol-IZ-um)
anxiety	(ang-ZY-uh-tee)
asexual	(AY-SEK-shoo-ul)
autonomic	(AW-tuh-NOM-ic)
carcinogenic	(KAR-sin-o-JEN-ik)
cirrhosis	(sur-O-sis)
compensation	(KOM-pen-SAY-shun)
compromise	(KOM-pro-myz)
conflict	(KON-flikt)
contraception	(KON-truh-SEP-shun)
culture	(KUL-chur)
delirium tremens	(di-LEER-i-um TREE-munz)
depressant	(di-PRES-unt)
diabetes	(DY-uh-BEE-tis)
distilled	(dis-TILD)
emotional	(ee-MO-shun-al)
endocrine system	(EN-do-krun SIS-tum)
environment	(en-VY-run-munt)
erection	(i-REK-shun)
essential	(uh-SEN-shul)
ethanol	(ETH-uh-nohl)
ethnic	(ETH-nik)
fermentation	(FUR-men-TAY-shun)
fertile period	(FUR-tul PIR-i-ud)
glands	(GLANDZ)
gonorrhea	(GON-uh-REE-uh)
heredity	(huh-RED-i-tee)
hormonal cycle	(hor-MON-ul SY-kul)
inconsistency	(IN-kun-SIS-tun-see)

inherited	(in-HARE-i-tid)
insulin	(IN-suh-lin)
intoxicated	(in-TOX-i-KAY-tid)
involuntary	(in-VOL-un-TARE-ee)
lethargic	(li-THAR-jik)
menstruation	(MEN-stroo-AY-shun)
narcotic	(nar-KOT-ik)
nationalities	(NASH-uh-NAL-uh-teez)
nervous system	(NUR-vus SIS-tum)
nicotine	(NIK-uh-teen)
nocturnal emission	(nok-TUR-nul i-MISH-un)
objectively	(ob-JEK-tiv-lee)
ovulation	(AH-vyoo-LAY-shun)
pancreas	(PAN-kree-us)
parathyroid	(PARE-uh-THY-roid)
peer group	(PIR GROOP)
personality	(PUR-suh-NAL-uh-tee)
physiological	(FIZ-i-uh-LOJ-uh-kul)
pituitary	(pi-TYOO-uh-TARE-i)
placenta	(pluh-SEN-tuh)
psychological	(SY-kuh-LOJ-uh-kul)
puberty	(PYOO-bur-tee)
repressed	(ree-PRESD)
security	(see-KYOOR-uh-tee)
self-esteem	(SELF- es-TEEM)
semen	(SEE-mun)
sibling rivalry	(SIB-ling RY-vul-ree)
siesta	(see-ES-tuh)
social situation	(SO-shul SICH-oo-AY-shun)
sperm	(SPURM)
stereotype	(STARE-ee-uh-typ)
steroid	(STARE-oid)
symbolic	(sim-BOL-ik)
syphilis	(SIF-uh-lis)
thymus	(THY-mus)
thyroid	(THY-roid)
umbilical	(um-BIL-uh-kul)
voluntary	(VOL-un-TARE-ee)
withdrawal symptoms	(with-DRAW-ul SIMP-tumz)